LINCOLN CHRISTIAN COLLEGE AND SEMINARY

W9-CCR-609

# Praise for
## *Entrepreneurial Faith*

"Kirbyjon Caldwell and Walt Kallestad are two of the most creative and entrepreneurial pastors in America. If you want to learn the secrets of entrepreneurial faith, these are the men to model yourself after. Their passion is inspiring, their faith is irresistible, and their advice is practical."

—RICK WARREN, founding pastor of Saddleback Church
and best-selling author of *The Purpose Driven Life*

"*Entrepreneurial Faith* is synergy at its best. Caldwell and Kallestad's work takes *Who Moved My Cheese* out of the maze by helping you not only understand change but lead it. Read it!"

—KEN BLANCHARD, coauthor of *The One Minute Manager*
and *The Servant Leader*

"*Entrepreneurial Faith* shows you how to join God in innovative and effective ministry. If you've seen enough of status-quo spirituality, use this guidebook to begin following the Great Entrepreneur."

—LAURIE BETH JONES, best-selling author of *Jesus CEO*,
*Teach Your Team to Fish*, and *Jesus, Entrepreneur*

"When you have faith in a big God, your life is full of exciting possibilities. *Entrepreneurial Faith* gives you the vision to see what God is doing in your community and then supplies the direction you need to get involved in meeting real needs in exciting and unexpected ways."

—DR. ROBERT H. SCHULLER, best-selling author, senior pastor
of The Crystal Cathedral, and host of *The Hour of Power*

"The philosophies and programs of many churches lag far behind the fast-changing communities in which they reside. If God's kingdom is to expand, entrepreneurial faith is required. Leaders need the humble ability to follow and trust a big God into uncharted waters so that value can be added to surrounding communities."

—TOM STEFFEN, coauthor of *Great Commission Companies*

"*Entrepreneurial Faith* tracks the profound shift from a traditional to a managerial and now to an entrepreneurial approach that is changing the face of American Christianity. Passionate and inspirational but also specific and actionable."

—BOB BUFORD, chairman and founder of Leadership Network and author of *Halftime: Changing Your Game Plan from Success to Significance*

# ENTREPRENEURIAL
# FAITH

## LAUNCHING BOLD INITIATIVES
## TO EXPAND GOD'S KINGDOM

## KIRBYJON CALDWELL
## & WALT KALLESTAD

### WITH PAUL SORENSEN

WaterBrook
PRESS

ENTREPRENEURIAL FAITH
PUBLISHED BY WATERBROOK PRESS
2375 Telstar Drive, Suite 160
Colorado Springs, Colorado 80920
*A division of Random House, Inc.*

All Scripture quotations, unless otherwise indicated, are taken from the *Holy Bible, New Living Translation,* copyright © 1996. Used by permission of Tyndale House Publishers, Inc., Wheaton, Illinois 60189. All rights reserved. Scripture quotations marked (KJV) are taken from the *King James Version.* Scripture quotations marked (NIV) are taken from the *Holy Bible, New International Version®.* NIV®. Copyright © 1973, 1978, 1984 by International Bible Society. Used by permission of Zondervan Publishing House. All rights reserved. Scripture quotations marked (NASB) are taken from the *New American Standard Bible®.* © Copyright The Lockman Foundation 1960, 1962, 1963, 1968, 1971, 1972, 1973, 1975, 1977, 1995. Used by permission. (www.Lockman.org).

Details in some anecdotes and stories have been changed to protect the identities of the persons involved.

ISBN 1-57856-837-4

Copyright © 2004 by Kirbyjon Caldwell, Walt Kallestad, and Paul Sorensen

All rights reserved. No part of this book may be reproduced or transmitted in any form or by any means, electronic or mechanical, including photocopying and recording, or by any information storage and retrieval system, without permission in writing from the publisher.

WATERBROOK and its deer design logo are registered trademarks of WaterBrook Press, a division of Random House, Inc.

Library of Congress Cataloging-in-Publication Data
Caldwell, Kirbyjon.
    Entrepreneurial faith : launching bold initiatives to expand God's kingdom / Kirbyjon Caldwell and Walt Kallestad with Paul Sorensen.— 1st ed.
        p. cm.
    Includes bibliographical references.
    ISBN 1-57856-837-4
    1. Church work.  I. Kallestad, Walther P., 1948–  II. Sorensen, Paul, 1956–  III. Title.
    BV4400.C28 2004
    253—dc22

                                                                        2004002880

Printed in the United States of America
2004—First Edition

10  9  8  7  6  5  4  3  2  1

We dedicate this book...to all the pastors and Christian leaders who live by entrepreneurial faith, to all who will follow Jesus and become entrepreneurial believers as you read this book, and to the Ultimate Entrepreneur, our Lord Jesus Christ.

1/59 *

109953

# CONTENTS

# ACKNOWLEDGMENTS

**M**any thanks to the following people:

The Windsor Village Church family members who continue to walk by faith and not by facts. May your commitment both to Jesus Christ and to the community continue to glow passionately and practically. I love you!

The people of the Community Church of Joy who have taken the risk to dream God-sized dreams and have believed that Jesus Christ can perform incredible miracles among us. The Joy leaders and staff team who have stepped out in faith with us over the past twenty-five years. Special thanks to our servant-leader team—Tim Wright, Dottie Escobedo-Frank, and Wayne Skaff—for diligently praying for and living out this dream together. We thank God for you all!

Jeff Dunn, for his incredible, Spirit-inspired gift of crafting our thoughts into creative and comprehensible words. And Mark Gilroy, who faithfully flew across the country with this dream until it landed.

Ron Lee and the publishing team at WaterBrook Press, for believing in our project enough to invest their time, energy, and incredible talents so faithfully.

Our faithful assistants—Billie Ryum, JoAnn White, and Mary Kallestad—for their amazing ability to coordinate our schedules, plus the many meetings with collaborators, financiers, creative partners, and dreamers.

And for the patient and encouraging love of our families through these many years of dreaming new dreams for ministry and this book:

Kirbyjon's family: Suzzette, Turner, Nia, and Alexander.

Walt's family: Mary, Patrick and Shannon, Shawn-Marie, and Brian.

Paul's family: Carol, David, Nathan, and April.

# AN OPEN LETTER TO
# ENTREPRENEURS OF FAITH

Y ou have in your hands more than just another leadership or self-help book. You have the beat of our hearts. We are followers of Jesus who have never been interested in maintaining the status quo. We are pastors who are passionate about serving God and answering the questions our hurting communities are asking. We have learned that maintaining the status quo serves neither God nor the people that He loves.

That explains why we are sold out to the vision and practice of entrepreneurial faith. We never want to be limited by what already exists. We aspire instead to pursue what should be. We desire to be ambassadors of the Kingdom of God in the places where we live and serve. We want to be catalysts of radical, Kingdom-on-earth changes that enrich the lives of the walking wounded who live all around us.

We have been pastors for a combined sixty years, and we know from hard experience that "church as usual" is guaranteed to fail. Status-quo ministry will never meet the diverse and growing needs of hurting people. The role of the church has been so narrowly defined and lived out that too many churches have lost touch with the communities they are supposed to minister to. Most of us continue to devote our resources and our best thinking to organizational maintenance and to meeting the needs of the people we already have. We might collect money for foreign missions, but when it comes to *local* needs, most churches are blind to what is happening outside the church walls. There is a curious vision problem, a short-sightedness that limits most ministry to the internal faith community. There is nothing wrong with believers ministering to one another, unless ministry stops there and goes no further. We are convinced that God wants to rip off our blinders and turn us loose in our world.

If you attend a church regularly, or even periodically, you are likely aware that your church can do more to address needs in your community. If you catch God's entrepreneurial vision, you can become an agent for change within your church and community, as you help connect your church's mission with the needs of people outside the church walls.

Perhaps you are part of the business community, and your daily work makes you aware of opportunities to touch people's lives with the grace of God. In your line of work, you are constantly formulating strategies that match services to areas of need. As you work in the community, you probably notice areas of spiritual and physical need where a church could make a significant difference if only it had bold vision. If that describes you and others you know in the business world, you could become a partner in entrepreneurial faith, assisting your church in launching bold initiatives to meet spiritual and physical needs.

Or maybe you are a pastor with big dreams for your church to touch the lives of hurting people. But you might be leading a "status-quo" church that is uncomfortable with change and unaccustomed to ministry that moves beyond the walls of the sanctuary. You might feel that you can't share your visions and dreams, let alone pursue them. If that describes you, then listen to the urgent cry of our hearts: Give yourself permission to dream new dreams! Then boldly follow your dreams. When obstacles loom, ask yourself,

*What does God want my church to be and to do? And what does God want me to be and do that I haven't yet seen?*

These are two core questions of entrepreneurial faith. The life of spiritual entrepreneurship sees what others are blind to. A spiritual entrepreneur dreams of new realities that others find threatening. He or she identifies needs and opportunities and seeks new ways to meet those needs, with little regard for what has already been tried or has never been attempted in the past. So ask yourself: *What would I be doing right now if I knew God was with me and I could not fail?* Ask that question now, and stop to think about the answer. When the answer comes into view, ask just one more question: *Who or what is keeping me from doing that very thing?* In some cases, the answer might be yourself. Perhaps you have grown too comfortable, and you're reluctant to step out on faith. Or perhaps you're dying to get started, but you're hampered by a negative pastor or church board or other lay leaders who prefer the known to the unknown—to the detriment of the vision. Whatever your answer, think about stepping out on faith and what that means before reading on.

## Status-Quo Thinking Will Fail the Church

The world is changing too rapidly for us to continue doing things just as we have done them in the past. If you think your city is immune to the radical changes and monumental shifts in our culture, think again. The United States is no longer a Christian nation, if it ever was one. Past assumptions about spiritual needs and beliefs, religious attitudes and allegiances, no longer hold sway. All this means that the past ways of doing ministry no longer speak to the needs of most people. If we're doing what we've always done, we might be missing the opportunity to minister to those who need it the most.

Consider some facts about Americans and their changing beliefs. Two of the fastest-growing religions in the United States are Buddhism and Hinduism. The number of adherents in these religious communities increased by nearly 200 percent in just ten years—from 1990 to 2000. In contrast, the number of Americans who call themselves Christians increased a mere 5 percent during that same decade. In the same period, the number of Americans who no longer consider themselves religious *in any way* increased by 110 percent.[1]

Want more facts?

According to surveys conducted by various organizations such as the Barna Research Group and the work of Robert Putnam, author of *Bowling Alone,* Christian church attendance remains about the same as it has for the past four decades. Approximately 42 percent of Americans attend church at least a few times a year, not counting Christmas and Easter. That number has declined slightly from a high of 46 percent in 1960.[2]

So while the entrenched mentality of maintaining the status quo in the church resulted in a flat growth of semiregular attendance, other religions and the number of religious dropouts have grown among Americans at astounding rates. And that's the "good" news.

Here's the bad news. A 2003 Barna Research Group survey showed that nearly eight million Americans between the ages of eighteen and twenty-nine have dropped out of church, have stopped giving money to churches, and are no longer reading their Bibles.[3] While the number alone is staggering, the implications for the future of Christian ministry are frightening. A major segment of the next generation of leaders in this country is immune to typical church ministry and deaf to the conventional methods of presenting the gospel.

David Kinnaman, vice president of the Barna Research Group and director of the survey, said Christianity is not going to dry up and blow away—after all, there are still more than ten million twentysomething Americans who regularly attend church. The real issue, according to Kinnaman, "is how churches will respond to the faithquakes that are reverberating through our nation's young adults. The notion that these people will return to the church when they get older or once they become parents is only true in a minority of cases. More important, that reasoning ignores the real issue: Millions of twentysomethings are crystallizing their views of life without the input of church leaders, the Bible, or other mature Christians. If we simply wait for them to come back to church later in adulthood, not only will most of those people never return, but also we would miss the chance to alter their life trajectory during a critical phase."[4]

## READY TO TRY SOMETHING NEW?

If we can't reach this generation by remaining within the walls of the church, and all the signs indicate that we can't, then it's time for entrepreneurial faith initiatives. We *must* take the church to the community. And it's not just the twentysomething generation that is being missed. Look around your community and start making a list. There's the immigrant population, the teen population, those who have grown up with no Christian influence and thus no familiarity with religion, and many, many others. Very few of these people will ever be affected by what goes on during a church service, no matter how dynamic, upbeat, and relevant the service is. Those who are following Buddhism or Hinduism, those who claim no religion, those who have been wounded in life (sometimes, even by the church), the lost men, women, boys, and girls in your community will not typically venture into your church. They have no reason to think they'll find any answers there. They still have a tremendous need to experience the awesome reality of God's love, but they won't come begging.

Status-quo ministry says "open the doors and they'll come." That might have worked in the past, but it long ago lost its effectiveness. We can no longer just schedule church services and programs and wait for those who need God to show up. We must find creative ways to engage the nonchurchgoers in our communities. We must take the gospel out of the church and to the people. We must become entrepreneurs as we practice our faith. If we refuse to take this step, we run the very real risk of losing literally millions around us who desperately need and want to experience the love of God and who live right in our neighborhoods.

Whether you are a pastor, an involved layperson, or a businessperson concerned about the needs in your community, it's time to start dreaming about how God can use you in new ways. Ways that may be scary at times, but adventures that will be exciting as well.

God is working in the world, and He invites us to join Him. But He doesn't limit Himself to tried-and-true methods, and He never shies away from disruptive innovation. In fact, if you study Jesus's method of ministry, you could easily argue that God *prefers* bold, people-focused initiatives that fly in the face of convention. Jesus's entrepreneurship opened people's eyes to spiritual truth in startling, unsettling, but welcome ways.

When we act on our vision, change takes place. Risk taking is a big part of the package. Thus, we can move forward with courageous faith, entrepreneurial faith. Creativity and dreaming can become the norm and not the rare exception. God calls us all to follow Him in the risky, exciting journey of entrepreneurial ministry. We can't live as true imitators of Jesus without practicing this type of faith.

## A TALE OF TWO COMMUNITIES

This book tells the story of two communities. Both are important centers of commerce and opportunity. Both have many wounded people living within their borders. In each of these communities, there are many churches. Large and small. Rich and poor. Black, white, brown, yellow, multicultural. In spite of the number of churches, however, there are still many people who are spiritually lost, hungry, and dying. Too often status-quo ministry ignores these people. The hunger and lostness continue, and we devote little thought, planning, or action toward providing genuine solutions.

This book also tells the story of a revolution that is changing the face of America. The revolution was not launched by outside forces, but from within the hearts of men and women who will no longer settle for what has always been. This is a story of the entrepreneurial revolution, a sweeping force that is changing the landscape of business, individual lifestyles, family relationships, and—yes—even the church.

Any individual, any group, and any church or organization can do something big for God as we get involved in what God is doing. Entrepreneurial faith connects the individual's Monday-through-Friday life with practical outreach that meets human needs with the grace of God. It taps into the passion and expertise of the businessperson and the professional, the layperson and the pastor, and even the behind-the-scenes people who quietly want to utilize their skills, knowledge, and abilities to help expand God's Kingdom.

Anyone can make the shift from static, status-quo faith to bold, outward-focused, entrepreneurial faith. You will find your own passions ignited, and you will find that you can stir the spiritual passion of others, as you help form innovative partnerships to launch new ventures for God.

In the chapters that follow, you will encounter a practical but powerful blueprint to help people of faith move out of the sanctuary and into the neighborhood. This approach is described in Scripture, and it works with effectiveness in any locale. It works with equal force in organizations of any size and when launching any type of new ministry.

Our story is not geared solely for those in large churches, nor is it limited to those who make their living in ministry. The entrepreneurial explosion starts in the soul of an individual who lives in a city, suburb, or small town. That soul might have access to millions of dollars in capital or be so poor that the widow's last two coins look like a fortune. This book is for those who look at the darkness in their communities and long to light them up. For those who see wounds and long to bring healing. For those who see spiritual death and want to replace it with eternal life. It is for laypersons, pastors, executives, working people, mothers, fathers, concerned teenagers.

In other words, the life of entrepreneurial faith is for you.

# A FRESH START IN HOUSTON

## A Kirbyjon Caldwell Chapter

My story has been told before in my book *The Gospel of Good Success*[1] and in numerous magazine articles and television interviews. Here is the abbreviated version.

I grew up in a neighborhood with lots of personality, in Houston's Fifth Ward, one corner of which was known as The Bloody Fifth because of the frequent murders committed there on weekends. My parents provided an incredibly stable home for me in a low- to moderate-income community. My father, an entrepreneur, worked hard throughout the week as a tailor at his men's clothing store. My mother was a counselor in one of Houston's notable public high schools.

Virtually every Sunday, our family went to Mount Vernon Methodist, a church smack-dab in the middle of the Fifth Ward. That church was a light shining in the midst of a potential darkness. It was there that I met the Rock of my life, my Leader and Forgiver. It was there that I first began to see that God did not want His children to be set up high on a hill away from the ills of the world, but to truly be the church, to be a place of refuge for the sick and hurting, the poor and lonely. All of that I learned in that rough and real portion of the Fifth Ward.

## GETTING ON, AND THEN OFF, THE FAST TRACK

After graduating from public school, I was fortunate to attend Carlton College, a private liberal arts college in Northfield, Minnesota. After that I decided to pursue a graduate degree so I could earn a decent living. I earned my MBA from the Wharton Graduate School of Management (at the University of Pennsylvania). I then spent a year as an institutional bond salesman on Wall Street. Life was good, fifteen hundred miles and a world away from my hometown. I had my pick of just about any city in the nation to live and work in. With my MBA and breadth of experience, doors immediately opened. But I chose to return to Houston, not knowing—just then—that it was part of God's master plan for the calling He was about to issue.

I took a position as a fixed-income institutional bond salesman, set on a fast track to financial success. I had a potential income that was virtually unheard of for African Americans in the late 1970s, unless they were professional athletes or physicians. I drove a Datsun 280Z 2+2 to my office with a prestigious regional investment banking company.

So when I walked into my boss's office one year later to announce that I was quitting to go into the ministry, he was stunned. It had the same impact as if a successful politician were to stand up in the House of Representatives to announce that he was leaving office to pursue a career as an elementary school teacher. My boss could not believe I was "throwing away" all that I had invested just to be a preacher. I simply replied, "It's not something I decided. It's what God has called me to do."

I enrolled in the Perkins School of Theology at Southern Methodist University, completing the four-year course of study in less than three years. After graduation, I was given a choice of pastoring a fairly established church in a middle-class section of Houston or a struggling church on the "other side of town." I thought it would be better to have a blank board that I could write on rather than have to erase a bunch of stuff folks had already inscribed in the comfortable church. So I crossed the tracks to the other side. Doing so didn't make any sense to most of the people who knew me, but I had no choice but to answer the call God placed on my heart.

My first Sunday, in June 1982, I rounded the corner off Heatherbrook Drive and saw my new "home." It was a plain, yet somehow quaint, one-story building that clearly had seen better days. Two of the major Baptist churches in the area were growing, but the Methodists of the Windsor Village church had dwindled to just twenty-five members. It was a congregation that most in the denomination had written off. (I subsequently learned that if my leadership of this church had not resulted in a turnaround, the church would have been sold.)

This is where I learned how God works through entrepreneurial faith (even though I would not have classified it as "entrepreneurial faith" at the time).

## Following God, the Almighty Entrepreneur

When I parked my car outside Windsor Village United Methodist Church, there was no sign out front announcing the arrival of a new pastor. What I did see, however, was a For Sale sign in the lot next door. Windsor Village was selling the adjacent lot to pay off the church's expenses, including my predecessor's salary. Not exactly the most encouraging message I could have received that morning.

I opened the doors to the sanctuary, wondering what other surprises were in store. The walls were a faded brown, highlighted here and there with cobwebs. There was a piano and a small organ. And there was a pulpit and some pews. Nothing fancy, but it was all I needed—a place to preach and a place for the people to sit.

That first morning we "packed" nearly one hundred twenty-five people into the sanctuary, mostly friends and extended family, as well as the remaining twenty-five faithful members. We cleared out the cobwebs and had a great day of church. I felt at home that very first Sunday.

As the days, then weeks, passed, my anticipation grew that God wanted to do something special in this neighborhood. It would have been easy for me to coast through this assignment, waiting for the district to come up with a bigger, more secure church for me to lead. But that was not God's plan, nor was it my desire.

## WHAT ENTREPRENEURIAL FAITH IS NOT

This is a crucial point to understand: Entrepreneurial faith is not about numbers, not about growth plans, not about increasing the offerings. Entrepreneurial faith is not just for those who are looking for a way to convert their small congregations into megachurches. Entrepreneurial faith is all about confronting challenges and obstacles and believing that God is bigger than anything that tries to oppose His work. It is understanding that God's ways are not our ways. It is trusting that God's vision is clearer and brighter than ours, and that His timing is more perfect than ours. It demands courage to develop and implement bold strategies to accomplish new visions. In short, entrepreneurial faith is for anyone, pastor or layperson, in any size community, in any church, with any amount of resources—or lack of resources. It is about God, not about us.

And there's more. Entrepreneurial faith is not just about having a dream or receiving a vision from God. It is *acting* on the dreams and visions that God gives us. An entrepreneur implements ideas with new strategies as he or she pursues new visions. Look in the Scriptures. God's strategies for His prophets were new, sometimes confusingly so. Imagine having to marry a prostitute in order to show God's incredible grace to His unfaithful people. Hosea did that when he married the harlot Gomer. That's entrepreneurial!

I did not arrive that Sunday morning with some master plan for Windsor Village. I had no schematic diagram showing how we would grow and how quickly. We did not launch a building program or membership drive. I spent much of my time getting to know those faithful members who had stuck it out through the hard times. I also invested time in the neighborhood, meeting with families, community leaders, and business owners nearby. I listened to their stories and got to know their needs and hopes. And the more I heard, the more I knew that this was a place where God needed to move.

Some folks were looking for their slice of "the pie" (and some are still looking!). But forget something as small as "the pie." I thank the Lord for the fact that the Kingdom of God is a whole bakery! We have access to croissants, cakes, bagels, muffins, and, of course, all kinds of pies. In the Kingdom of God there is no lack, no scarcity, and no poverty. In the Kingdom of God there is justice, including economic justice and the creation of jobs so people can support their families. That is what God is up to in *every* place, not just in our part of Houston. Knowing that, the next question was "How could our church be a part of what God wanted to do in this community?" We needed to take the gospel outside the walls of our sanctuary and into the lives of those around us. But how?

Over the next ten years Windsor Village church grew even as the neighborhood around it remained steady. I began to love those who attended our church and to care for those in the community who went to another church or to no church. And for ten years, nearly every day as I drove to my office, I passed an abandoned building that once housed a Kmart. Right off Highway 90, this more than 100,000-square-foot empty box was a constant reminder that the boom had busted, at least in this corner of Houston. But I did not see the potential in that vacant building until I had a vision in the most unusual place—a Wal-Mart store in Jonesboro, Arkansas.

Standing there between housewares and hardware, the idea came to me. Why couldn't the people of God become a Wal-Mart of healing and grace to our community? Why couldn't we offer a variety of services, including medical, financial, educational, and emotional healing to our community? Why couldn't we offer these in the name of Jesus?

Prior to my Wal-Mart experience, Buster Friedman and the late Donald Bonham of Fiesta Mart, Inc., asked if we knew anyone in the community who could make good use of the abandoned Kmart building. I told him I would get back to him. When I began to feel God direct my heart to better serve our community, I realized why this real estate expert had come to me. The Holy Spirit was orchestrating this entire affair. I presented the dream to some folks in our church, and I shared with members of a Bible study about the empty Kmart and how the real estate professional was looking for someone who could use it to help the community.

"How about us?" someone asked. Those in the Bible study could see more clearly at that time than I could. They immediately thought of the jobs that would be created if that center could be revitalized. And when people have jobs, then they can better care for themselves and their families. Healthy people constitute healthy families. And healthy families constitute a healthy community. Before I knew it, we were planning how best to use that huge empty building. We were walking as entrepreneurs, marrying a challenge with a vision to create a blessing for others. We decided to call our new place of opportunity The Power Center.

The Power Center now houses the University of Texas Science Center; Memorial Hermann Hospital health clinic; Houston Community College business technology center; Imani School; a Women, Infants, and Children (WIC) center; and a branch of J. P. Morgan Chase Bank of Texas—the *only* bank in our neighborhood. There are private executive business suites, a pharmacy, a beauty salon, and the fourth-largest banquet and convention facility in Houston—all housed in what had been nothing more than a huge empty building.

The Power Center provides employment for more than 250 people and pumps approximately $15.5 million into the local economy annually. These are good, honest people working hard, serving others, and providing for the needs of their families. This awesome project is a reality because of God's grace, Fiesta Mart's generosity, and the people's desire to do something great for the community. This is entrepreneurial faith in action.

## ENTREPRENEURS ARE ALWAYS DREAMING

While we were excited about what the Power Center was doing in our city, we didn't consider our job finished. I, as well as the like-hearted persons I had asked to be leaders around me, continued to pray and seek ways we could be the hand of God outstretched to our corner of Houston.

A few years ago, we were looking for a tract of land where we could eventually build a prayer center. We needed about twenty acres for the type of structure we had envisioned. I frequently drove past a large plot of land, much more than we would ever need. But my wife (smart men listen to their wives!) suggested I call the owner to see if he would sell us twenty acres.

It took two weeks to track down the owner, and when I called he said he wasn't interested in selling. "And if I *did* want to sell it," he continued, "I would sell the whole 234 acres or nothing. I'm not going to mess around with subdividing it."

"But we don't need that much land," I countered.

"That's a personal problem," was his response.

So I gathered the Pyramid CDC team and selected members from the church, and we began to seek God's will for the land. As we prayed, an idea came to us. *Houses.* Houston, like many major metropolitan areas, has a great need for first-class (and I do mean First Class), affordable housing for those who for one reason or another cannot get a house of their own. So we purchased the entire tract of land and, working as our own developer, we have completed three building phases with a total of 452 single-family homes. Three factors may have contributed to the seller's decision: (1) the compelling vision, (2) the eleven-month negotiating process, or (3) the Lord touched his heart. Former Secretary of Housing and Urban Development Mario Cuomo said Corinthian Pointe is the largest residential subdivision ever built by a nonprofit organization. There are some people living in these homes who, a year or two previous to moving in, were literally homeless.

On this 234-acre tract, we are also developing a YMCA, a satellite of the Houston Museum of Natural Science (the fourth most visited museum in the nation), the Zina Garrison Tennis Center, a community park, an amphitheater, a commercial shopping center, an independent living facility, and a commercial catfish pond.

In addition to these projects, we will develop the 450,000-square-foot Kingdom Builders' Center (KBC). The KBC will include a prayer center; a sanctuary; fellowship areas; a family life center; an aquarium mall; a bookstore, cafe, and floral-shop complex; a carousel; a two-story slide; a chapel; a skating arena; and a parking garage. Entrepreneurs know the value of land, even if it is undeveloped. As a matter of fact, some entrepreneurs *prefer* undeveloped land. They are all about developing nothing into something useful and profitable, adding value, and changing lives.

We took each of these steps in faith, bathed every step in prayer, and evaluated each step strategically. We do not blindly stumble forward, but neither do we shy away from great challenges. Entrepreneurial faith is a daily adventure. We don't rest on our laurels. We look for hurting people, for new, effective ways to meet their needs, and for opportunities to improve the quality of life.

Always remember that we follow and serve the Almighty Entrepreneur, who calls us to a life of faith that dreams big, pursues the vision that God gives, and acts boldly. The life of faith takes risks to get the gospel out of the sanctuary and into the neighborhood. As you consider your own community, remember that an entrepreneur marries a challenge with a vision to create a blessing for others.

Now let's hear Walt's story.

# A FRESH START IN THE DESERT

## A Walt Kallestad Chapter

K irbyjon eventually found his way back to his hometown after college and graduate school and the life of high finance on Wall Street. My life took a different path, leading from frigid Minnesota to the desert of Arizona. And while Kirbyjon gained incredible experience in the business world before entering full-time ministry, I sensed God's call to be in the ministry as a young child. Then during my teens and early twenties, I did not sense God's call. Finally, at the great age of twenty-seven, God's call compelled me to full-time ordained ministry. But there is one important thing that Kirbyjon and I share in common: We both have an insatiable desire to reach hurting people with the message of God's grace.

I had just received my master of divinity degree from Luther Seminary in St. Paul, Minnesota, when I arrived in Phoenix as the new pastor of Community Church of Joy. It was a ragged campus with a congregation to match. Weeds obscured the sign in front of the church, and even if you found the right entry for the parking lot, you had to avoid a pothole in the driveway that was big enough to swallow a Volkswagen. Talk about risk-taking.

I was so grateful for this opportunity, and I certainly wanted to serve those who made Community Church of Joy their home. But I also knew that God had called me to position the church in a way that would welcome those who had no church home. I wanted to create an atmosphere so that those who were unfamiliar with Lutheran liturgy and jargon would still feel connected with God. I thought those who already called this church their home would welcome such a shift in emphasis.

I couldn't have been more wrong.

When I arrived, the church had two hundred members. Within twelve months, I had grown the church all the way to one hundred people. We had the fastest-declining congregation in the entire denomination. I could have led seminars on the most effective methods for losing members, but no one asked.

The other leaders of the church began holding meetings in homes, devising ways to get rid of me. Our church treasurer told me, "Every time you open your mouth, Kallestad, you cost us money!" And just when I thought things couldn't get any worse, they did.

It was a Wednesday evening, and I was having dinner with my family. In the middle of dinner, I received a call from the dispatcher at the fire department telling me the church was on fire. As I hung up the phone, my first thought was, *Let it burn*. I went to my car, but before I could start the engine I began crying. I felt like such a failure. I cried out to God, "If you want me to get out of ministry and out of this place, I'll go."

Instead, He gave me entrepreneurial faith.

## CATCHING FIRE FOR THE KINGDOM

The fire in the church kitchen was quickly contained. But the fire God ignited in my heart burned out of control. I knew that if I were to succeed as a pastor, it was going to be because of God's power flowing through me. A level of excitement rose within. *What in the world is God going to do?*

I saw that, for that first year as pastor, I had been acting as a fireman. I was constantly putting out one flare-up after another. It seemed I spent all my time and energy on problems. So I knew a change was needed. I decided to look for opportunities that I could pursue rather than fires to try to contain.

In his book *Effective Church Leadership,* Kennon Callahan wrote, "The day of the professional minister is over—the day of the missionary pastor has come."[1] This was the vision I needed. I had to stop looking at myself as a professional minister, constantly putting out the blazes that sprang up in our church. I had to see myself as a missionary pastor, reaching outside the church's walls to those who were so battered and bruised by life that they could not care for themselves. And I had to find a way to get our church to think in the same way.

Early in my second year of ministry, those who remained at the church gathered to help craft our vision statement. We started with a clean slate and crafted what would set our course for the next two-plus decades. We felt a cry in our hearts to reach the lost and dying in northwest Phoenix. We wanted to shout,

> All who have not heard the gospel or who have rejected it in the past, you are welcome here.
>
> All who are staggering under unbearable burdens, you are welcome here.
>
> All who are in any kind of need, or are without hope, you are welcome here.
>
> All who wish to be a part of a community where Jesus is our Captain and everybody is somebody, you are welcome here.
>
> All who want to be a part of a passionate vision, and not just a church, you are welcome here.

This was—and still is—our heart's cry.

## Gearing Down for Slow Success

I'd like to say that as soon as we clarified our mission we were overrun with new members and had to build a bigger sanctuary. But that wasn't the case. For the next several years we saw steady growth in the number of members. But more than that, we saw depth developing in those who connected with Community Church of Joy. A core group within the church began inviting their friends to come with them. We observed more and more people reach out to the unchurched in their circles. We were launching our mission of taking the gospel outside of our walls to those who needed to hear it.

I volunteered to be the chaplain for a high-school football team. After the games on Friday nights we would open the church for the team, their friends, and any other teens who wanted to come for pizza and a movie. Soon, some of these teens began attending our Sunday-morning services. Then their parents came with them. This is just one small example of how we began to minister to our community. But even with such a small start, God started blessing our initiatives.

As we pursued new ways to get the gospel out of the sanctuary and into the community, we met with the mayor of Glendale (a suburb of Phoenix) and business leaders in the community to see how we could best help. Those with entrepreneurial faith look beyond the walls of their surroundings and into the whole community. We are not to ignore the homeless, the helpless, the disenfranchised. Entrepreneurial faith is not given so we personally can *have* more, but so that we can *give* more to others.

## More Land, Not Less

When I arrived at Community Church of Joy in 1978, the church owned ten acres. I was told to sell seven acres in order to repay monies owed to the denomination for the startup mission fund. But I protested, saying we would need *more* land, not less. I wanted to buy four more acres that were available adjacent to our property. Once you sell land, it's gone. Be careful how you manage the purchase and sale of your land for the purpose of maximizing your ministry. You need to look for ways to grow, not stay the way you are now.

Instead of cutting back, we cut loose. At the time this was a huge commitment on the part of our people. We only had a few hundred members, but they sacrificially stepped up and raised $272,000 to buy the land.

Within the first few years of my pastorate at Community Church of Joy, we developed our fourteen-acre campus, building a nine-hundred-seat sanctuary to replace our original three-hundred-seat fellowship hall. But after adding five more weekend worship services over the next ten years, the larger sanctuary proved to be too small. If people thought I was crazy when I said we needed four more acres adjacent to our original ten, imagine what people thought of me when I said we needed to look for ten times the amount of land that we had!

Who in their right mind would suggest buying more than one hundred acres for a church? Well, a person with entrepreneurial faith would.


## The Heart of Entrepreneurial Faith

I use land as an example of asking God for a vision, putting the vision in front of others, and then following that vision in faith. The goal of entrepreneurial faith is not more land, not bigger sanctuaries, not a larger congregation. The heart of entrepreneurial faith is the hearts of individuals. We are interested in, just as God is interested in, transformed hearts. Yes, Community Church of Joy got its land, 127 acres of prime property that was far beyond our wildest hopes or dreams. But through this process we saw something even greater happen. We watched God change the heart of a man.

In search of land to grow on, we found a grove of orange trees that was perfectly located in what demographic surveys indicated would become the center of metropolitan Phoenix within the following two decades. It was easily accessible from the new highway, Loop 101, that circles Phoenix and

Scottsdale. And you could see the land clearly from the highway. This was the perfect location.

We found out that the property had recently been purchased by a developer who had a reputation for being a ruthless negotiator. Tony Nicoli had no interest in talking with a preacher about selling the orange grove. His assistant refused to put my call through after she asked me one question: "Do you have any money to buy this property?"

When I answered no, that ended the conversation.

But I kept calling, trying to get her to understand the vision we had for reaching out to this corner of Phoenix. It did no good. Here is an important lesson: Your vision is *your* vision, not anyone else's. Don't expect others to automatically buy into what God has put on your heart. Others can't see what you see if they don't share your heart—a heart that has been changed by the love of God through the power of Jesus. If you don't believe me, just look again at the prophets of the Old Testament. Not many of these men and women received a warm welcome when they shared their vision.

Tony Nicoli not only didn't give us a warm reception, he didn't even give us the time of day.

Finally, I called his secretary once more and asked if she would ask Tony to come check us out next Sunday. Just give us a chance.

One Sunday not long after, I was up front sharing the message for the morning when I saw the door open in the back of the sanctuary. A tall, well-groomed man walked in, stood there for a few moments, then quickly left. I knew it had to be Tony Nicoli!

I called his secretary the next Monday and said, "Thank you for passing on the invitation to Tony. He came to our service yesterday, and I would like to talk with him to see how he liked it."

She was shocked! But she did put me through to him. After a short conversation, we set a time to meet for lunch. It was then I shared my dream, how we wanted to use the land to make a difference in the community. We wanted to bring healing and hope, in the name of Christ. Tony was very moved. I invited him to come back to church to worship with us. The next week, he came once again, this time with his wife, sitting in the back row. I called the next day to see what he thought of the service.

"Oh, we liked it," he said. "We don't know much about God, but we'll be back."

And they did come back. Each Sunday they moved closer to the front. One week at the end of the message, Tony arose from his seat (now very near the front) and walked toward me. I could see that his eyes were moist with tears. He asked if he had to be born again to go to heaven. I said, "Yes, but I'd like to talk with you more about it. Can we meet for lunch?"

So we had lunch together for a second time. I explained how God loved him so much He sent His Son to pay the ultimate debt for our sins. Tony then recounted to me all the things he had done throughout his life.

"There's no way God could forgive all of that," Tony said.

"Yes He can and will," I said. We prayed together in the restaurant. Tony's heart was transformed that day. A short time later, his wife told me that she was living with a new man. It was Tony, but the change in his life was astounding.

After that, Tony was open to talking with us about the land. He saw our vision for reaching our community. But we still had a problem. We didn't have the money it would take to buy his prime acres. God, as usual, came up with a most creative solution. He used the seller to help provide the funds for the buyer! Tony gave us nearly a quarter million dollars to buy his land. He helped us in the process of negotiating and purchasing the property. Tony owned 634 acres on this site. He brought in sewer and water, then sold the lots to home builders. There was a huge demand for the lots, but Tony set aside 127 acres that the developers could not buy. He was keeping it for us. And just before we moved into our new church home on the land Tony sold to us, he died of an aneurysm. A few months later, his wife passed away from cancer. I am sure Tony and Betty are enjoying what they are seeing through heaven's eyes.

## A DELIGHTFUL LESSON OF ENTREPRENEURIAL FAITH

Entrepreneurial faith results in great blessing to those outside the church who need to be touched by the grace of God. But there is great blessing as well for those already in the Kingdom.

At the Community Church of Joy, God gave us a vision for reaching the community, and we knew it would require a lot more land than we had. When we ran into Tony Nicoli, he seemed to represent an insurmountable hurdle in our ability to buy this land. At the same time, if we had drawn up a composite description of the person we wanted to reach with our ministry, it would have been Tony Nicoli. A needy man who at first didn't acknowledge his need, but over time came to admit his utter need for God and His forgiveness.

And God used this very man to provide the property for the ministry that reached him with the gospel of grace. Only God could imagine such a creative solution!

# PART I

## JESUS, THE ULTIMATE ENTREPRENEUR

# THREE

# TRAIN WITH THE BEST

## Jesus Turned the World Upside Down in Just Three Years

He grew up in the family business, learning His trade from His dad. Hour by hour they worked to fulfill orders, the Son at first watching, then helping, then managing His own projects. His father smiled with pride when the Son finished His first piece by Himself. It was most likely a chair or possibly a small table. It was crafted well, especially so for a boy who was not yet ten years old.

By the time He was twelve, however, the boy knew that carpentry was not His calling. He could feel the stirring in His soul. He began watching and learning as He prepared for the mission that He was on this planet to complete.

He remained in the carpentry trade until He was thirty, running the business after His dad died, more than likely training His younger brothers just as He had been trained. His eye for design showed He was an artist as well as a craftsman. The pieces He produced were built to last and were in high demand. As the village carpenter, He was counted on to build and repair furniture and tools used every day. He also used His ability to make gifts and decorations that helped the oppressed people of His land find a glimmer of hope, as they lived in an occupied territory, ruled by a foreign power.

But as good as He was in creating wonderful and functional things out of wood, carpentry was not His ultimate destiny. So at the age of thirty He retired from the carpentry business and set out on a new venture. He was troubled by the deep needs of the people around Him and knew that the existing methods fell far short of meeting those needs. He listened to the teachers of religious law and tradition and knew that their techniques failed to bring about heart changes in those who heard the teachings. He yearned to help the lost, to gather them to Himself as a good shepherd would gather wandering sheep.

So He left everything that was familiar, the safe and secure family business. He set out alone at first, with no means of livelihood and nowhere to live. Soon He gathered around Him passionate but untrained coworkers, and in three years this Entrepreneur and His ragtag band of followers started a movement that changed the world.

## An Entrepreneur Without Equal

Jesus of Nazareth was, and is, the Ultimate Entrepreneur. That may sound like a false characterization, especially if you think of entrepreneurs only as people who are gifted in making money. Jesus, of course, was not about turning a tidy profit.

But that doesn't mean that He wasn't the consummate Entrepreneur.

We're not saying Jesus came to earth to secure patents, to build corporations, and to take His company public so He could make a killing on the IPO. Frankly, He didn't need the money. He had already owned everything before He left heaven and took on human form. He chose to set everything aside and enter the noise and dirt and turmoil of life on earth to fulfill His heart's desire—to save men and women from death brought about by slavery to sin. Jesus was the Ultimate Entrepreneur because He looked at the way things were and refused to allow them to remain that way. He set the standard for entrepreneurship.

An entrepreneur, in the best sense of that word, is one who is not satisfied with the way things are and who refuses to stand on the sidelines doing nothing about it. A true entrepreneur is not primarily about making money, but about using his or her skill and expertise and knowledge and passion to make life better for others. An entrepreneur is one who finds a niche, seizes the opportunity, and adds value to the community.

One of the earliest definitions of *entrepreneur* had nothing to do with money. Austrian economist Joseph Schumpeter's definition emphasized innovation, including new products, new manufacturing processes, and new uses for existing products. He talked about galvanizing human capital for new enterprises.[1] We believe entrepreneurship is about *seeing, sizing,* and *seizing* opportunities. This means taking on challenges in a new way—acting boldly and taking risks—while expecting new results that improve people's lives. Change stands at the heart of entrepreneurship. If you risk nothing more than what you've always done, you'll get nothing more than what you've always gotten.

## THE NEW AND NECESSARY WAY

At the time Jesus began His entrepreneurial ministry, Jewish society was held captive by Roman oppression. The Roman Empire tolerated Jewish culture and traditions, but the Jewish leaders longed for freedom from foreign rule. Throughout Israel's history a pattern had developed where the nation would turn from God and then be conquered or taken into captivity by another nation. In bondage or exile, they would long for their freedom or their homeland and would repent and turn back to God. Then God would deliver them from captivity. This pattern repeats itself several times in the Old Testament.

In Jesus's time, the Jewish nation was crying out once again for deliverance.

Two prominent groups approached the problem in two different ways. The Pharisees—the religious rulers of the day—tried to manipulate God. They felt that if they were careful to follow the letter of every law, God would have no choice but to answer their prayers. By extension, if they could get every Jew to obey God completely, then God would have to deliver the nation of Israel. It was an attempt to control God and His actions by slavishly obeying Him, even in the smallest detail.

Then came a group of radical extremists—Zealots, they were called—who thought the best hope for Israel's liberation lay with a military coup. The extremists were looking for a Messiah, a mighty deliverer who would come brandishing a sword. Such a figure would bring Rome to its knees and put an end to the foreign occupation of Judea.

As different as they were, the Pharisees and the Zealots both represented the status quo. They both gave their all to pushing the same agenda they'd been behind for years. And they both were coming up short. Nothing was changing.

Then came Jesus, a figure like no other, the promised deliverer of Israel with a completely new agenda. He knew His calling, He had a clear vision of the future, and He refused to follow either of the established paths.

Instead of focusing on the obstacle of Roman occupation, Jesus saw opportunities. He knew better than anyone that nothing short of a completely new way would bring about the change that was needed.

Jesus stepped outside the religious and cultural mainstream when He went public with His message. There were many others preaching revolutionary ideas—the zealots included—but their efforts were political in nature, focusing on establishing the kingdom of Israel as an independent nation. Jesus pointed His followers away from political solutions and toward the Kingdom of God. Other teachers worked within the system the Pharisees had established, seeking a way to twist God's arm through absolute obedience to His commands and by conforming to human-made religious traditions. Jesus boldly pointed out the hypocrisy of this approach, telling His followers they had to have *much higher* standards. After all, entrepreneurship is the *new* way, not the status quo.

Jesus taught His message through ordinary means, such as parables, preaching, and object lessons, just as many other teachers—or rabbis—did in the first century. But being an entrepreneur, Jesus couldn't help but turn the system on its head. Instead of the traditional method of teaching that deferred to other, authoritative teachers, Jesus used Himself as the authority. He often was heard to say, "You have heard that the law of Moses says.... But I say..." (Matthew 5:21-22,27-28,31-32,33-34,38-39,43-44). Speaking so was risky, a completely new way of doing things. What if the people rejected this unorthodox method of teaching? Everything could fall apart pretty quickly. All His hard work would come to nothing.

But Jesus knew what He was about, and the reward was great. The people who heard Him teach could conclude nothing other than this: *We have never heard anyone teach with such authority!* (see Matthew 7:28-29).

# FOUR

# JESUS, THE CONSUMMATE ENTREPRENEUR

## Follow the Original Blueprint for Entrepreneurial Faith

If you're still not convinced that Jesus operated as an entrepreneur, let's look at His life and see what it shows us. Here are five distinct ways that Jesus created the original blueprint for entrepreneurial faith.

### HE CHALLENGED EXISTING MINDSETS

When Jesus began His earthly ministry, the prevailing teaching about God was that He was a harsh taskmaster, and in order to please Him you had to strictly follow every part of the Mosaic Law and even the established religious customs and traditions. As you can imagine, these expectations created incredible feelings of guilt and inadequacy among those who wanted to follow God.

Then Jesus arrived and turned things around. "You have heard that the law of Moses says," He cried. "But I say…" Jesus challenged not only the teachings of the religious leaders of His day but the leaders themselves. Jesus knew that trying to follow the Law and human tradition led to nothing but endless frustration. So He proposed something completely new.

Jesus came with a new contract without tearing up the old contract (required obedience to God's Law). Instead, He fulfilled the Law for us by living on earth and fulfilling to the smallest detail all of God's Law. Then He offered us a new deal: He forgave our debts, freeing us to live life to its fullest potential. Not only was this a new deal, it was the *perfect* deal. He even gave us His Holy Spirit to help us live in this faith relationship. Entrepreneurs look at things the way they are and say, "It doesn't have to stay like this. There *has* to be a better way." To get new results, it's necessary to challenge existing mindsets. Just the way Jesus did.

## He Introduced Kingdom Initiatives

Jesus's followers continually asked Him the same question—even after His resurrection: "Is this the time when we get to shake off the shackles of Roman rule and run Israel ourselves?" (see Acts 1:6). What they didn't understand was that Jesus had already freed them from human rule and introduced them to a new kingdom—the Kingdom of God. When you live and operate in God's Kingdom, you are subject to His rule—no matter who the human rulers might be.

Jesus taught that the Kingdom of God was not some distant dream world but a Kingdom we can live in right now. It is where God's will is done. It is where we can feel safe and secure, even when the oppressors are shouting and shaking their spears at us.

Entrepreneurs introduce new rules and new conditions for living. They don't accept what everyone else sees as reality. They look for a new reality behind what is seen by others. They go deeper to discover the truth that sheds light on what is masquerading as the truth. They probe and investigate and consider alternatives. They develop new initiatives to bring the truth and power of God's Kingdom to bear on our temporal world.

## HE UPENDED THE STATUS QUO

Status and social standing mean everything to some people. Seating arrangements are a perfect indication of this, revealing the people who think more of themselves than others think of them. If there's a formal dinner, they're convinced they merit seats at the head table. They deserve them, since they are more powerful and more important than others in the room.

Such thinking is perfectly acceptable to those who subscribe to a human system of measuring worth and assigning value. Jesus, the Entrepreneur, taught differently, establishing an upside-down standard. He said, "Start at the back of the room and wait for someone to call you forward." He taught His followers that, instead of cutting to the front of a line, the best place to begin is at the back of the line. Then, He said, when things are turned upside down, you'll end up in the front (see Luke 14:7-11).

As every entrepreneur knows, adhering to the status quo will get you only what you've already had in the past. If you're out to change things, to improve lives, you've got to adopt the methods of Jesus. A spiritual entrepreneur is never afraid to turn things upside down, to challenge the accepted authorities, to find the truth behind what sells itself as the truth, and to take initiatives based on what he or she discovers.

## HE INCREASED HIS FOLLOWERS' CAPACITY

It does us no good to receive more of anything if we're not ready to handle more. Most of us have enough trouble handling what we already have. So Jesus goes to work to help us accept and properly use the increase He wants to give us. He strengthens our fishing net so that when we, in obedience to

His command, throw it into the water on the other side of the boat, we can haul in the overwhelming catch that He brings.

So many people have a reverse understanding of what it means to allow Jesus to direct their lives. Following Jesus does not mean losing all the things He "makes us give up." It's just the opposite. Following the Lord is all about what He gives us. It's about the abundance we receive as we live in obedience to His vision, His guidance, and His plans for us. He is the only One who can deliver a future, real hope, health, and life!

Entrepreneurs of faith prepare others for the Kingdom of God and get them ready to receive the increase that is coming their way. Who would refuse a chance to be part of such a venture?

## He Added Value

Entrepreneurs look at current products and services and evaluate them to see how value can be added. Likewise, Jesus looked at life around Him and saw how He could add value. He brought eternal value to ordinary human life.

To the woman who met Him at the well, a woman who endured social ostracism and who lived in immorality, Jesus added living water (see John 4:1-26). To those who were blind, Jesus added sight (see John 9:1-25). To Zacchaeus, the corrupt tax collector, Jesus added real wealth (see Luke 19: 1-10). To Lazarus, Jesus's close friend who had died, Jesus added life to his days (see John 11:38-44). As we learn from the consummate Entrepreneur, we find that the practice of entrepreneurial faith today can produce results similar to those of Jesus. In fact, He told His followers that they would do even greater things than what He had done on earth (see John 14:12-14).

Spiritual entrepreneurship challenges existing mindsets, introduces Kingdom initiatives, upends the status quo, increases capacity, and adds value. Jesus showed us how these things are done, so that we can step out in faith and follow Him.

## THE MODEL THAT WE FOLLOW

Entrepreneurs follow Jesus's blueprint and take bold risks to advance God's Kingdom. Working through the Holy Spirit, God continues to launch bold initiatives on earth. In establishing His Kingdom, God reaches out to us again and again with His love. Whenever God draws us to Himself, He is acting in response to our need. As we enjoy the benefits and blessings of His work in our lives, we're getting a real taste of needs being met by an entrepreneurial God. This is the model we are called to imitate in our own life of faith.

We have been promised the mind of Christ, and that is a promise we all need to claim (see 1 Corinthians 2:16). Entrepreneurial faith is not ultimately about techniques and strategy; it's about following God. He is "able to accomplish infinitely more than we would ever dare to ask or hope" (Ephesians 3:20).

Jesus continues to call us to join Him in changing the world. He is looking for those who will follow Him in an incredible journey of entrepreneurial faith. So let's get started.

# FIVE

# THE ENTREPRENEUR PROFILE

## It's Time to Locate Your Community

O n the street that ran alongside the old German church in a Chicago neighborhood, the National Guard tanks and trucks rolled by to squelch the riots that had erupted, disrupting the entire city. Those riots of the late 1960s and early 1970s left the West Garfield Park community in shambles. Homeowners, landlords, banks, businesses, and investors fled this West Side neighborhood. In their wake came poverty, unemployment, and despair. No longer could the German Lutherans hide safely within their church.

Yet instead of giving in to despair, these faithful and faith-filled believers took to the streets. Members of Bethel Lutheran Church decided to fight the poverty and hopelessness. In the late 1970s they invested their meager resources to buy and renovate a three-flat apartment building. In doing so, they gave birth to Bethel New Life.

Since 1979, Bethel New Life has earned a national reputation for cutting-edge initiatives and pioneering approaches that serve the community. They have built upon the people, physical assets, and faith base of the community. Bethel strives to turn problems into possibilities through community efforts that arise out of a commitment to self-help and self-determination, brought about by solution-oriented initiatives.

Within a few city blocks of this African American community on the West Side of Chicago, they operate multiple programs, including supportive housing for families who teeter on the edge of homelessness. They launched a gang-violence prevention team and founded a school and a day-care ministry. Ten years ago Bethel New Life converted a worn-out city hospital into a cultural center, with senior housing, a child development center, medical offices, a credit union, and a community business center.

Bethel now employs nearly 350 people with 1,200 additional volunteers who donate 7,700 hours of their time each year. These efforts have brought more than $110 million in investments into this once-undesirable community. More than 1,000 new affordable housing units have been built, and 7,000 people have been placed in living-wage jobs.

From a riotous beginning an oasis of hope has arisen. This is entrepreneurial faith in action.[1]

## THE PROFILE OF AN ENTREPRENEUR

Entrepreneurial faith requires looking at your community, your ministry, your relationships, and your entire life in a completely new way. It embraces opportunities to step out of the usual into the exciting and, yes, sometimes into the scary. It's living life on the edge and loving the view. But before we go any further, let's establish a working definition of what we're talking about. In other words, how does entrepreneurial faith work?

In the business community, an *entrepreneur* is most often defined as "an agent of change," "a person who adds value," "one who moves forward with creativity and passion," and "a person who is comfortable with risk." While all of these phrases fit the normal definition of entrepreneur, they fall short of what we're talking about. When you consider immersing yourself in the life of entrepreneurial faith, you are anticipating a total transformation— leaving the comfortable status quo to become a person who is a change agent, adding value through creatively and passionately launching bold initiatives, all the while taking calculated risks *for God.* Those last two words are crucial. Serving God in entrepreneurship is what sets our work apart from a business venture or a financial enterprise. The work of entrepreneurial faith is done on earth, but it is spiritual in nature. It is done by humans guided by God, and it produces eternal results.

To streamline the definition further, consider this understanding of a person of entrepreneurial faith: anyone who sees what God wants him (or her) to see, believes in what he sees, and does it. We're all entrepreneurial when we're seeing, sizing up, and seizing opportunities for God.

The person who pursues this life launches initiatives that respond to real needs, takes advantage of opportunities that fit the vision that God gives, creates services that meet real needs, and—most important—affects lives that are destined for eternity. While some of the strategies overlap with entrepreneurship in the business world, the goal far surpasses anything you'll ever accomplish in a business enterprise. The goal is nothing short of expanding God's Kingdom on earth.

If this entrepreneurial life sounds daunting and completely undoable, or merely naive, let us stress that the life of entrepreneurial faith is not a solitary venture. The key to succeeding in this risky venture is enlisting and joining forces with a group of like-minded comrades, gifted and passionate general- ists and specialists who help define your mission, help assess needs, analyze opportunities, and work together in meeting human needs and ministering in your community.

## LOCATE YOUR COMMUNITY

The first Kiwanis club was formed in Detroit, Michigan, in 1915 to provide a setting for exchanging business contacts. But club members in the Motor City quickly began doing more than just networking to expand profit opportunities. They started providing social services for the needy around them. By 1919, Kiwanis officially adopted the service model for its national charter. By 1960, Kiwanis membership numbered close to one million in the United States and Canada.

Today, membership in the service organization has dropped by nearly 40 percent. And this is not the only national club to see its membership decline drastically. The Jaycees have experienced a 58 percent decline; the PTA, a 60 percent loss; and the American Red Cross has seen 61 percent of its volunteers disappear since its peak.[2]

Robert Putnam, the Malkin Professor of Public Policy at Harvard University, has explored the disappearance of "social capital," referring to human values such as trustworthiness, acceptance, mutual aid, and networking, which we experience as a society. "Beginning, roughly speaking, in the late 1960s," writes Putnam, "Americans in massive numbers began to join less, trust less, give less, vote less, and schmooze less."[3] He notes that over the past thirty-plus years, membership in churches, as well as civic and social clubs, has fallen by 25 to 50 percent. "A variety of technological and economic and social changes—television, two-career families, urban sprawl, and so on—has rendered obsolete a good share of America's stock of social capital," Putnam concludes.[4]

As we discuss entrepreneurial faith, we will refer to "community" rather than "social capital," although both terms refer to people banding together. In the life of entrepreneurial faith, Christians band together to identify opportunities and then use their passion and expertise to meet the needs of those around them. The work of spiritual entrepreneurship is done as a community.

But the recipients of this bold ministry are also in a community. The communities of people who need the touch of God's grace, through the work of His people, can be considered any gathering of people around a common theme, be it geographical region (neighborhoods and towns), vocation (our workplace), education (the parents of our children's classmates), hobbies (garden clubs, bowling leagues), or any number of other lifestyle categories. We each live in several communities, interacting daily with our "neighbors" in these groups. Community includes the people we associate with regularly, those we share life with.

## COMMUNITY IS GOD'S IDEA

But why is community so important? For starters, God purposefully places each of us where we are—geographically and relationally. He wants us to be salt and light in this world. He delays His work of separating the wheat from the weeds, choosing instead to let the wheat live next to the weeds. As we live in these communities, we have the privilege of introducing the life-giving and life-changing Kingdom-of-God principles to those who live in a flawed and fallen world where stealing and cheating, greed and violence, competition and destruction rule the day.

The entrepreneurial-faith community is called to reach out to these other communities, the communities that surround us and that we inhabit through our various involvements. According to Professor Putnam, those who attend church regularly "are much more likely than other people to visit friends, to entertain at home, to attend club meetings, and to belong to sports groups."[5] In other words, those who are more serious about their faith are the same people who seek out others and form community with them. But why are followers of Jesus drawn to serve, to share, to give? What drives them to act as entrepreneurs in reaction to the needs in their various communities? Is it, as Putnam says, simply that churchgoers know more people and thus become aware of more opportunities? This is certainly part of the answer.

But we are convinced that the complete answer lies much deeper. We believe that Christians, those born into new life by the grace of God and the Holy Spirit, bear in their beings the heart of Jesus. And we believe that Jesus, at His core, is the Ultimate Entrepreneur who goes into all communities to meet and care for the needy.

"Love your neighbor," Jesus taught, "as you love yourself" (see Matthew 19:19). Neighbor and self, a small community of care, an opportunity to take the initiative to demonstrate God's grace to others.

But who qualifies as your "neighbor"? The Pharisees who were listening to Jesus had the same question. But their curiosity didn't arise from a sincere desire to understand His teachings. Instead, they were trying to trip Him up. "Let's nail this upstart on what He means, exactly, when He says 'neighbor,'" they must have said among themselves. "Either it will be so broad as to have no real meaning, or it will be so narrow that we can find loopholes that will relieve us of any real responsibility to serve others."

But Jesus, as always, cut to the chase: Your neighbor is anyone who needs your help (see Luke 10:25-37). Thus, we encounter our neighbors every day. We can't avoid it. And we shouldn't want to avoid it.

Every one of us resides in a community that is populated by needy people who hunger for God's touch. Some don't recognize the source of their hunger, but they know the hunger exists. It takes entrepreneurial faith to show our neighbors the One who can relieve our hunger.

# SIX

# YOU'RE CRAZY!

## And Other Signs You're Going in the Right Direction

I t is said that people resist few things more than change. Even when making a change promises to improve conditions for all involved, those affected by it still experience anxiety. We find security in familiar surroundings, even if those surroundings aren't entirely to our liking. Leaving the familiar for the untested makes most people uneasy.

But others thrive on change, so they sometimes have trouble understanding why so many resist it. If efficiency and productivity can be enhanced and service improved and profits increased, then go for it! What's the problem?

The problem is that change involves risk, and most people are uncomfortable with risk. That probably explains why many churches continue to maintain the same programs and ministries that have been in place for years, even when the communities around the churches change with younger families moving in, or with more kids living with single parents, or with governments' cutting back on social programs. The needs are constantly changing, but sadly the ministries usually remain the same.

The person committed to a life of entrepreneurial faith—whether a pastor or layperson, a business leader or worker—is an agent of change. No matter what they do for a living, entrepreneurs will embrace the chance to take advantage of new opportunities.

Changing worship style seems to disrupt a community of faith more than any other element. Just try forgetting the "Doxology" one week (or, if your church does not sing the "Doxology," add it in) and see what happens. We are routine-oriented people. "New" is not always "improved." Just recall what happened when Coke changed its traditional formula. But change is a constant in our lives, and every change creates new opportunities. It's times of change that get entrepreneurs excited. Their attitude is: Routines create ruts, and the only difference between a rut and a grave are the dimensions.

So why, besides the risk factor, do people resist change? At a recent seminar, best-selling author and international management consultant Margaret Wheatley said, "The primary issue among leaders today is fear and anxiety. When we become fearful, we stop thinking. We become internal. This, in turn, creates more chaos within." Fear creates resistance to change.

Another underlying issue for status-quo people is control. Wheatley observed that recent studies show that organizations built on teams, rather than relying on hierarchical leadership, are 35 percent more productive. But most corporations in America do not embrace a team concept, even though productivity is supposedly the goal. This is true in the church as well. We want to be effective in outreach to our communities, but we're reluctant to release control.[1] But a spiritual entrepreneur, being a change agent, is willing to release control to achieve a vision.

In fact, a spiritual entrepreneur *provokes* change by creating opportunities. He or she will introduce a new idea or a new way of utilizing an existing ministry or church program just to get people thinking "change." Entrepreneurs do not have to be inventors, however, creating something completely

new, such as the modern-day equivalent of the wheel. Instead, many entrepreneurs are innovators, finding new and exciting ways to use what already
exists. The wheel is useful for transportation, but also is central to the operation of any number of amusement park rides. The wheel is commonly used
as a steering device, but also can be used as a gear, as a pulley, as a spool, as a
measuring device, and for any number of other purposes. The entrepreneur
looks at a common wheel and sees not a wheel but a marvelous circular
device that can be utilized in a tremendous variety of ways to improve the
lives of people.

Entrepreneurs have the ability to see far beyond an item's current use.
They identify opportunities and possibilities that others miss. They make
small changes to a product or process to meet whatever new need might arise.


## FIVE NOT-SO-CRAZY CHARACTERISTICS

While entrepreneurs impact all types of organizations, they all share common
characteristics. First, entrepreneurs focus on what can be, not on what is.
They approach challenges as opportunities for launching new initiatives.
Whenever an entrepreneur sees a need arise or an obstacle appear—in a product, in the economy, in society as a whole—he or she investigates to see how
to meet that challenge. Entrepreneurial thinking never settles for "as is."

Second, entrepreneurs are disciplined. They identify their mission and
keep that in front of them as they assess opportunities. While they have passion to pursue new opportunities, they don't waste time and resources on
ventures they know they're not called to. They don't dilute their efforts by
following every opportunity. Disciplined entrepreneurs may be involved in
several projects at once, but they look for links between them to best use their
time, money, and energy.

Third, entrepreneurs know when to pull the trigger to say go rather than
continuing to calculate the risks. Entrepreneurs know it's sometimes more
costly to be slow than to be wrong. Perfection is not the goal. And because

plans can and will go awry, entrepreneurs are able to quickly adapt to new circumstances as things develop and change.

Fourth, entrepreneurs are artists more than engineers. They are leaders more than managers. They capture possibilities rather than getting mired in current reality. Entrepreneurs are creative, players in the game rather than coaches on the sidelines. They sit in with a weekend jazz band rather than conducting an orchestra. Entrepreneurs let their imaginations take them places that the typical thinker would never explore. Dreaming big is never a waste of time for the entrepreneur. On the contrary, it is the heart of entrepreneurship. An entrepreneurial organization may never be the best in its field, but it is likely to be very good in several related fields and, thus, be very successful.

Finally, entrepreneurs burn with passion. They pursue new opportunities with single-mindedness and zeal. The hours to launch a new venture can be endless, and the rewards—at least in the short term—meager. If there's no passion, if the new opportunity becomes simply a job, such a scenario does not fit the picture of an entrepreneur. Those who have an entrepreneurial mindset wake up excited about conquering the unconquerable. Entrepreneurs love the journey as much as the end result.

Innovation, pursuing opportunities, pulling the trigger, seeing the possibilities, and living and working with passion. All of these lead to change—something an entrepreneur can't help but create. The same traits are true of spiritual entrepreneurs. Expressed differently, the entrepreneur of faith dreams big, sees possibilities not limitations, burns with passion to meet needs, enlists and leads others in the cause, knows his or her mission, and innovates to maximize the effectiveness and reach of existing programs and ministries.

## From a Stork or a Book?

Are entrepreneurs born or made? The answer is yes. Some are born with an insatiable appetite for new ventures, constantly seeking new obstacles to conquer. These men and women typically are more creative than the average person and more expressive in their thoughts and ideas. It's easy to follow the lead of such persons because they make even the difficult paths fun to travel.

Then there are those who are more analytical in their thinking. To these persons, no problem can't be set down on paper, diagramed, charted, made into an equation, and given to a committee to solve. Yet even for these analytical thinkers, there comes the day when a challenge presents itself and even the best charts and the most careful calculations fail to present a solution. The analyzer then reaches to take a different approach, a creative one, to solving the problem. It works! He or she is, if even for one moment, an entrepreneur.

The truth is, we all are entrepreneurs. Some of us go there intentionally, others by being mentored, and others because we were born to live this life. But we all at one time or another come up with new, untried solutions when presented with a challenge or an unmet need. Traveling on the road less traveled is not the most comfortable path for some, but it's a road we all follow at times. And it's the best description of the life of faith.

Even if you see yourself as being more at home with diagrams and charts, you can pursue the life of entrepreneurial faith. If you are sparked with a passion to expand the Kingdom of God, you can become a spiritual entrepreneur as you seek to fulfill God's calling in your life.

# PART II

---

# THE LIFE
# OF THE SPIRITUAL
# ENTREPRENEUR

# SEVEN

# INVESTING YOUR LIFE
# FOR THE HIGHEST RETURN

## Enjoy a Better Payoff Than Safety and Comfort

There was a poster that was popular in the 1970s. It showed a beautiful sailboat on a choppy sea. The caption read, "A boat in a harbor is safe, but that is not what boats are built for."

You may be enjoying the safety of your harbor after years of struggle and hard work. Perhaps you finally achieved a major goal, so why would you want to sail back into the rough waters of entrepreneurial ministry? Obviously, we entrepreneurs think the rewards make the risks worthwhile or we wouldn't live the way we do.

No one can deny the appeal of comfort and safety. But they're not the greatest goods in life. Trouble and danger, while never welcome in themselves, bring lessons and rewards that don't come any other way. With that in mind, here are a few great reasons why you should prayerfully consider pursuing an entrepreneurial lifestyle.

## You Can Join God in Shaping Your Future

Most people misbelieve that life is what happens to them, not what happens through them. When you pursue the life of entrepreneurial faith, you can to an extent shape your future rather than simply accepting whatever comes along. You don't have to abide by the axiom that "God loves you, and your church board has a wonderful plan for your life."

That is where I (Walt) found myself in my first year as pastor of Community Church of Joy. I had been spending much of my time meeting with people who were not members of our church—getting to know them and learning about their needs. When that came to light, I was told that I was wasting my time and that I should get back to what the church members expected of me. In other words, the church board wanted me to invest my efforts in taking care of those who were already members of the church. Insiders took priority over outsiders.

I listened to their suggestions, realizing I was accountable to them, but I made the choice to follow the mission statement crafted by the church: *That all may know Jesus Christ, and become His followers, we share His love with joy inspired by the Holy Spirit.*

I decided that God wanted me to spend significant time with people outside my congregation. So I continued investing in those who needed God but didn't realize it just yet. By following God's vision, I found freedom from the relentless day-to-day demands. I realized that I didn't have to cave in to the preferences of a few people in my congregation. God's vision came first, which freed me to pursue my calling without guilt and without giving in to outside pressure.

Entrepreneurs sometimes have reputations as renegades, and we need to recognize that rebellion against authority is a dangerous thing. But to live in obedience to God, we must line up our hearts with His calling and the needs of our community.

## YOU CAN CONTROL THE TIME CLOCK

An entrepreneur can, to a great extent, set his or her own time schedule. Be aware, however, that when you start a new venture, your schedule may consume all 168 hours in the week! Being an entrepreneur calls for hard work. So if you're going to be a healthy, long-lived entrepreneur, you must learn to live a balanced life. What does it profit you if you gain your vision but lose your equilibrium?

Living in balance doesn't detract from the thrill of entrepreneurship. In fact, if you're truly pursuing the life of entrepreneurial faith, there's no escape from the adventure. You plan a strategy and move ahead, only to find that the journey takes an unexpected turn—usually lots of them. This just gets your juices going even more. There is greater joy and excitement when you're living on the edge of faith.

## YOU CAN RELEASE YOUR CREATIVITY

As an entrepreneur, you are free to express your creativity. When you launch a new venture, all bets are off. You don't have to stick to the way it's always been done. In fact, entrepreneurs seldom give much thought to the way things were done in the past. If it's not working, then why waste time repeating it?

God is the Creator of the universe, and He gives each of us a measure of creativity. It's one of the human traits that reflect the image of God. One of the great joys of entrepreneurial faith is that we are freed to release this gift from God. Entrepreneurs aren't caught up in limitations. We prefer possibilities. So release your creative passion. Unfurl your sails and head for the harborless horizon.

There's an incredible thrill in making something out of nothing. That is what spiritual entrepreneurs do!

## You Can Cross Conventional Boundaries

Managers organize and maintain. Entrepreneurs innovate and expand and create. You don't have to live in maintenance mode. Your church board, or your staff, or those with a years-long stake in the enterprise might pressure you to expend your energies keeping everything in place and operating as usual. But an entrepreneur isn't interested in the usual. He or she is looking for the *unusual*, the delight of the unexpected, the satisfaction of finding ways to address needs and meet those needs in ways never done before.

When you move outside the boundaries you find great rewards—and great risks. It's always amazing how, when we live beyond our limits, stretching beyond what we ordinarily do, we see God's provision. We don't see His abundant provision ahead of time. Why would He give it when we aren't out there beyond the breakwater, where we need it the most? We move forward in faith, then He comes along providing just what we need. When we keep the boat in the harbor, we rob ourselves of the experience of seeing God provide in amazing ways.

The entrepreneur of faith invests his or her life to reap the highest return. And since this is entrepreneurship to meet others' needs, the return is not indicated by the bottom line. The return is seen in the spiritual realm, in the lives of the people in your neighborhood. Entrepreneurs are not just productive, they are reproductive. When you invest your life in others, the fruit of your labor will be seen for generations to come.

## You Can Find New Power and Wisdom in the Scriptures

The Bible is God's written revelation, reliable and authoritative. That is orthodox Christian doctrine, and it's a belief Christians have shared over two millennia. But if you settle for mere belief, you're cheating yourself and those God has called you to serve.

When you dive into the life of entrepreneurial faith, you come to know God's truth in a new way. It's no longer simply good principles and solid moral teaching and interesting facts about God. Now it's a source of direction, inspiration, insight, and solutions. It helps you stay on course when others oppose you. It encourages you when you're about to lose hope. It gives you strength when you've run out of your own. It reassures you that God is a Partner in the process, that you're not alone, that your calling has not changed.

Bottom line: When you are a spiritual entrepreneur, you are obeying God. You are engaging in the lives of the people God loves, rather than remaining a spectator in the stands. The promise in Joel, repeated in Acts, is that the young will see visions and the old will dream dreams (see Joel 2:28 and Acts 2:17). According to Scripture, being an entrepreneur is for everyone.

If this life is for everyone, then that includes you. God made you who you are and put you where you are for a reason. You have a divine calling. God has a mission, and you're a part of it. It won't be easy, but who wants easy? Try exciting, joyful, adventuresome. That's the life God wants for you. That's the new life of entrepreneurial faith.

# EIGHT

# THE NEW WORLD
# OF AN ENTREPRENEUR

## Opportunities That Come Disguised
## As Trouble

If you have decided to leave behind the safety and comfort of life in the harbor, let us give you one more assurance that you have chosen the right path. The life of entrepreneurial faith reflects the character of the Lord God Almighty. God created the universe out of a formless void. Talk about starting from scratch. He created humankind and enjoyed free and open fellowship with them in a breathtakingly beautiful place. Then sin entered the picture, and it was clear that a change was needed. The humans chose estrangement from God, so He set into motion a plan for human redemption. Talk about innovation.

And God is the biggest risk taker imaginable. He created humans so He could love them and be loved by them. He wanted to delight in the people He created, and He wanted them to delight in His company. But He also gave them the freedom to make their own choices. They could choose to reject Him. Can you imagine Almighty God allowing weak humans a choice in such an important matter? What if they decided that paradise wasn't good enough—that God's companionship somehow didn't provide all the goodies they were looking for? They might decide to reject Him.

And most did. God took a gamble, and some might say He lost. But ultimately He won. As the first Entrepreneur, He set in motion a divine strategy to bring us back to Him, to reconcile us to Himself after we turned our backs and chose disobedience over relationship with Him. In bringing us back to Himself, God provided the best model possible of spiritual entrepreneurship. So as we seek guidance and direction on this adventurous path, we need look no further than God's example.

Today, when we follow God's lead in entrepreneurial faith, we are entrusted with a calling to extend the Kingdom of God on earth. God wants to break into every person's world. As we make ourselves available, God will use us to advance His Kingdom. Entrepreneurial faith accomplishes God's will on earth, just as His will is done in heaven.

Think about this: We imitate God when we devote our lives to entrepreneurial faith.

## ENTREPRENEURIAL EXECUTION

Once a follower of Christ catches the vision that faith is, by nature and by definition, entrepreneurial, he or she can begin asking God for a vision that will put such faith to use. Many of the principles of business entrepreneurship apply to the life of faith, but the goal is very different.

In his westerns, Clint Eastwood's character is always an entrepreneur. He's always looking for trouble. Instead of noticing injustice and just ignoring it or heading in the opposite direction, he seeks it out and then finds a way to beat it. He doesn't just sit back and let life pass by. And he doesn't change course to avoid the hard path so he can find a more comfortable life.

He sees what needs to be done and then takes the initiative. You might think Eastwood was merely portraying a nearly silent gunslinger in those early spaghetti westerns, but he was really giving us a picture of an Old West entrepreneur.

None of us likes trouble, but it's a reality of life. And even if we can avoid it today, it will reappear tomorrow or next week. So we might as well confront it. But as we do, let's use the eyes of an entrepreneur. Look for opportunities that are hidden within trouble. This is a practice common to entrepreneurs—whether in the world of business or working in the Kingdom of God. Let's look more closely at how entrepreneurs operate.

## Trouble Is Good

An entrepreneur is not put off when something goes wrong with a product or service. If it happens once, it's no problem. But if it occurs often enough, then a change is needed. An existing process or part in the mechanism will need to be fixed. Now things are looking up.

Entrepreneurs live to fix things. Remember Tim "The Toolman" Taylor on television's *Home Improvement*? He was always looking for ways to improve things that didn't work the way he thought they should. He constantly tinkered with household appliances to make them better, to add "more power." Usually his improved product ended up exploding or catching on fire, but he kept trying. He had the heart of an entrepreneur.

Entrepreneurs are not troubled by trouble. Their reaction is "Let's find a way to make it better!"

## Passionate About New Challenges

Most people prefer that things stay the way they've always been. Familiarity gives them a degree of security. But experience tells us this will never be reality, so it's better to become an entrepreneur who welcomes change. Entrepreneurs know that right around the corner from trouble is an opportunity to find new and better ways to do things.

Entrepreneurs stay alert for disruptions in the way things are normally done. How about you? If you attend a more traditional church that you love, how did you respond when you first heard your church was going to institute a new type of worship service? Did you rejoice over this new opportunity to reach people in your community with the gospel, or did you complain that it was not what you've always done? When you found out a new bar was opening in your neighborhood, did you complain to the zoning commission and arrange for protestors to line the sidewalk with picket signs, or did you immediately start thinking of ways you could minister to the patrons of the bar? After all, they're looking for community and a listening ear. Those people need to know that the church has just what they need. Or at least it *should* have what they're looking for. How you react to change says much about whether you have the mind of an entrepreneur.

## Just Do It

Entrepreneurs not only seek out new opportunities, they take action once the opportunity becomes clear. While some will analyze every aspect, run risk assessments, and crunch numbers until their eyes glaze over, entrepreneurs, to quote a famous brand of athletic shoe, "just do it."

Entrepreneurs understand that opportunities are fleeting. Waiting until everything is just right will often guarantee that the opportunity disappears before you decide to take action. And if there still is a chance to seize the opportunity, you may find that it's now more complex or more costly than it would have been if action had been taken much sooner. Entrepreneurs value forward movement, so they get started—knowing they'll have to redo something or fix a few things along the way. That's all right. You can correct things as you learn. After all, a well-oiled machine doesn't just appear overnight.

This is not to say that you should rush into situations blindly or that you should avoid doing the right amount of research before you commit yourself to a project. But being an entrepreneur is like being an explorer—there are no guarantees about what's ahead, except that it will be exciting.

## Failure Is an Option

For Gene Kranz, NASA mission commander during the Apollo 13 moon flight, failure would have meant the death of three astronauts and, perhaps, a fatal blow to the space program. He told his group of flight engineers, assembled to try to find a way to get Jim Lovell, Fred Haise, and Jack Swigert safely home, that "failure is not an option."[1]

Fortunately for entrepreneurs, failure not only is an option, it is *expected*. Entrepreneurs do not, of course, *try* to fail. But neither do they run from opportunities where they might fail, even when the possibility of failure seems to others to be remarkably high. Entrepreneurs move forward, and if things don't work out, they learn from failure, build on it, and grow from it.

Success does not mean avoiding failure. Success for an entrepreneur is simply not giving up. Those who are still standing when the bell rings are the winners.

## Inspire the Vision in Others

An entrepreneur knows that he or she can't make an important difference working alone. It is by getting others to buy into the vision, by engaging others in the activity, that the mission moves forward.

Entrepreneurs create an atmosphere of expectation within an organization. The expectation generates energy, a force that will keep work moving forward when difficulties arise. And difficulties will most definitely arise. Spiritual entrepreneurs burn with passion and spiritual intensity. Entrepreneurial faith begets more entrepreneurial faith. Once one person catches the passionate fire of change, others will be infected.

## LESSONS FROM THE YOUNGEST ENTREPRENEURS

Knowing the risks and difficulties that are inherent in the life of an entrepreneur, it would be easy to lose heart and decide it's not worth the hassle. So let's look at the foundation of this way of life. As complicated as Kingdom work can become, it's amazing that it works best when it is based on simplicity and trust. The greatest entrepreneurs alive are found setting up shop in yards outside the homes of the poor, the middle class, and the wealthy in every town and city across the nation. On hot summer days, these entrepreneurs reach out to you with a smile and a product you can't resist. Even if the lemonade is too strong or too weak, too sweet or—oops!—no sugar added, you thank them and gladly give more than the asking price.

Children are great models of entrepreneurship in action. Whether they are running lemonade stands, washing cars, walking dogs, or mowing lawns, children know what adults find so hard to understand: Entrepreneurs simply see a need and then find a fun, creative way to meet it.

For some reason, kids absorb this concept without making the challenge more complicated or difficult than it is. Children don't look to add more tedious labor to their lives. For some reason, as we grow older we think something needs to be difficult or a struggle in order for it to have merit. Kids easily do what they love and figure out how to *avoid* what they don't like to do. Even when faced with chores when they would rather be outside playing, children find ways to make the work fun, often by coming up with new ways to complete a task.

Children naturally gravitate to what's new. They aren't put off by change. How do your kids react when you tell them the family is taking a vacation to a place they have never visited before? Do they complain that the family isn't going back to Toledo to visit Uncle Sid like you have for the past five years? Do they get grumpy because a trip to the Grand Canyon isn't "what we've always done"? Or do they smile and clap their hands, expectant at the promise of new adventure, even though they know almost nothing about the destination? New is not frightening to a child—it is exciting!

And there's one more lesson about entrepreneurship we can learn from kids. They instinctively know that entrepreneurship is a team sport. They spend a lot of time dividing up tasks to complete the work with the least pain and bother, rather than bowing to the orders of a dictator. They don't act as a top-down organization, with one child coming up with all the ideas and the rest simply doing the work. That structure wouldn't last very long among the kids we know. As a matter of fact, the talking out of the idea and delegating tasks seems to be just as much fun as the actual carrying out of the task. Watch kids when they gather for a game of sandlot football. Drawing up plays in the dirt is as big a part of the game as running, blocking, passing, and swarming to the ball. Children enjoy the whole journey.

How differently would we act if we could be kids again for just one day? How much more creativity would flow from our conference rooms if crayons and construction paper were substituted for spreadsheets and a slick Power-Point presentation? What if we actually got excited when we thought of making a change and doing things in a new way? Imagine what it would be like to have just as much fun doing the work of God's Kingdom as it is seeing the end result.

Imagine having the entrepreneurial faith of a child. We're serious. Spend some time imagining just that.

# NINE

# THE REVOLUTION THAT EXPANDS GOD'S KINGDOM

## Rethinking Entrepreneurship and the Church

I t's not too much of a stretch to say that Bill Gates brought about the fall of Communism. Or that Craig McCaw was responsible for the destruction of the Berlin Wall.

Gates and McCaw are recognized leaders of the great entrepreneurial revolution that defined the last quarter of the twentieth century. Some have called it the greatest revolution since the founding of our nation. Entrepreneurship changed the economic and social structures of the United States. And the shock waves of that revolution have been felt around the world.

While Gates was busy building Microsoft into the world leader in computer software, and McCaw drew from the assets of his small cable television enterprise to create the first nationwide cellular telephone network, those living behind the Iron Curtain were beginning to awaken to the idea that they, too, could create better lives for themselves. It was not weapons of warfare that brought about the fall of the Soviet Union and its satellite states. The Cold War was ended by the weapons of entrepreneurship, the philosophy that anyone with a vision and focused passion could create a business that would serve the community and open the door to greater income opportunities. After the Berlin Wall was reduced to a pile of rubble, it was entrepreneurs in East Germany, not the government, who began rebuilding their neglected country.

And certainly we can see the influence of entrepreneurial leaders in the dotcom craze of the 1990s. Companies that were born in a garage or a college dorm room led to twenty-two-year-old CEOs and the stock market run-up. Even when the dotcom bubble burst, these innovators didn't retreat to desk jobs. They are back in their garages (now located in much nicer neighborhoods) coming up with the next "killer app."

Entrepreneurs continue to be the driving force of the U.S. economy. Where the nineteenth century was led by a handful of major corporations, the late-twentieth century—and now the twenty-first century—has been dominated by small companies, sometimes run by just a single person, with a new twist on a product or service.

This entrepreneurial revolution has given birth to products and services that we consider essential to daily life, including personal computers, biotechnology, cable television, WiFi, cell phones, convenience foods, personal fitness, personal finance, and, of course, the Internet.

## NONPROFIT ENTREPRENEURS

At first, the term *nonprofit entrepreneurs* seems to be an oxymoron. But inasmuch as one definition of an entrepreneur is *one who creates new ways to make money*, and nonprofit organizations need revenue to operate, the phrase makes perfect sense. Now, nonprofits don't pocket any profits; they reinvest them or use them to launch other charitable ventures. Nonprofit does not mean you have to lose money. But that often is the case. We are in a time when many social organizations are fighting for their survival.

Let's make a distinction here. A nonprofit manager focuses on the survival of the organization. In addition to that, a social entrepreneur focuses on helping individuals and communities by bringing about cultural change. Social entrepreneurs seek to make the world a better place by fulfilling a social mission. The social entrepreneur has bifocal vision—seeing what the organization should become and galvanizing potential to add value. Social entrepreneurs are innovative, resourceful, and opportunity oriented.

An ever-increasing number of organizations are seeking a piece of a quickly shrinking donor base. If you lead a nonprofit organization, you have to find new ways to do more with less. Competition for donor dollars, the cost of soliciting and collecting those dollars, and even competition from for-profits entering the social sector all are pressing in on you. Yet the needs of those you serve aren't going away. You need help in the form of entrepreneurial faith. Entrepreneurial thinking is not only helpful, it is *essential* for nonprofits to survive in these times.

The traditional leader of a nonprofit organization looks at the shortage of donations and tries to find a way to get more money from his or her donors, and to find more donors. Good luck. In contrast, the *entrepreneurial* nonprofit leader sees that the problem is not a lack of donors, but a lack of money to do what he or she is called to do. "Forget finding new donors," this leader says. "Let's find new ways to fund our mission."

That's just what the Delancey Street Foundation's homeless facility in downtown San Francisco is doing. The foundation serves the needs of more than one thousand former substance abusers and ex-convicts with facilities in Los Angeles, New Mexico, North Carolina, New York, and their headquarters, San Francisco. Their main source of income (making up 60 percent of their revenue in 2001) is from the Delancey Street Restaurant, one of the most popular and critically acclaimed restaurants in San Francisco. Not only do they rely on income from the restaurant to fund services, but those who are using their homeless facilities turn their lives around in part through learning new vocational skills by working at the restaurant. This is entrepreneurial faith in action.

## THE LEGACY OF ENTREPRENEURIAL FAITH

The idea of funding Christian service and ministry through nontraditional means is not a new one. We can see the origins of this model in past centuries in the life of the church.

In seventeenth-century Germany, Christians settled for simply *doing* church, rather than seeking new ways to *be* the church as commanded in Scripture. They assured themselves that their doctrine was correct and that the influence they held over people's lives was complete. Getting involved with needy people in a way that would dirty their hands was not on their agenda.

So, when the citizens of Halle realized they had no money for food, they sent their children into the forest. They had spent their last few coins on alcohol, which also was now gone. So they told their children to look for food, knowing they would die from the cold and the weakness brought on by malnutrition. The told themselves they would not miss them, though, at least not as much as they missed their drink.

Their church knew of this condition. They also knew about their desperate children, as the church was aware of so many other children they had buried. But incredibly, the church chose not to get involved.

Then a man named Phillip Jakob Spener decided he could no longer look the other way. He and a group of followers, known around Halle as Pietists, set up orphanages to take in abandoned children. The Pietists established small groups where love and grace were more than just words. They were actions that saved the lives of the hungry and neglected. They created schools for orphans with such excellence that the Princes of Denmark sent children to these schools. Spener and Pietist followers became the social activists of the seventeenth century. Their methods were copied by other believers throughout Europe and were brought by immigrants to the New World.

Entrepreneurialism—responding to need in new and creative ways—is what drives a church to *be* the church. Entrepreneurial thinking and action is not only effective in the business and nonprofit worlds. The church must embrace entrepreneurial faith in order to reach the hungry and neglected of our world. If today's believers are ever to *be* the church rather than simply *doing the business* of church, then entrepreneurial faith is no longer optional!

This is not an idea that began in the seventeenth century. In the book of Acts we see the early church involved in the needs of the surrounding community. If the church today were really being the church and fulfilling its mission as set forth in Acts, if we were taking the sanctuary to the streets, we would have less crime and violence in our towns and cities. We would have fewer people living without direction in their lives, resorting to drugs or gangs or antisocial behavior. We would have less alcoholism, less domestic abuse, fewer broken families.

Getting involved in our communities is not just a nice idea. It's not optional. It's the reason the church exists. If you don't believe us, read the book of Acts. Inspired and empowered by the Holy Spirit (see Acts 1:8 and 4:31), the early believers shared their wealth for the sake of those in need (see Acts 4:32-35). As they served widows and orphans, they innovated and selected a team to create and organize a food program (see Acts 6:1-4). As they shared, the Lord multiplied their numbers.

## BUT WHY NOT TODAY?

American churches in recent decades have not typically approached the life of faith as an entrepreneurial venture. We can think of a couple of reasons for this failure to *be* the church.

First, until recently, the concept of entrepreneurship has been narrowly associated with financial success within a business framework. Most Americans see religious faith and business enterprises having little or nothing to do with each other. Pastors see themselves (and rightly so) driven by spiritual and social goals before financial ones. So church leaders focus on incrementally improving existing ministries rather than launching bold new initiatives.

The second reason the church is not actively entrepreneurial is that once a ministry has been started and takes on a life of its own, it separates from the church and, often, drifts from the church's emphasis on spiritual matters. Look at some of the great hospitals in our cities. Many were founded by churches to administer both physical and spiritual care. Once these hospitals grew to where they had their own means of financial support, they became separate entities from their founding churches, and spiritual accountability was lost.

Yet the concept of an entrepreneurial church, a church that is active in both the spiritual and physical aspects of its community, is rooted in the earliest history of the Christian church. Early monasteries depended on commercial ventures such as agriculture to support their needs and to provide finances to minister to the poor. The Jesuits felt God's passion to help people learn to read and write in order to become leaders in their communities. They set up farms to fund educational outreaches, resulting in some of the greatest schools in the world.[1] The Moravians planted profitable enterprises alongside their churches, because they knew that offerings from their congregations alone could not sustain their mission churches.[2] They viewed these mission-based enterprises as ways to help people in their communities develop skills that would allow them to prosper. Generating revenue in this way not only funded charitable enterprises but also served as a practical method of training the community in marketable skills.

Throughout history, churches have been leaders in entrepreneurial efforts. Many cities have nursing homes, substance-abuse programs, and adoption agencies that are outgrowths of church ministries. Until recently, many—if not most—community programs were started and operated by churches. We need to once again take the church to the streets. We need entrepreneurial churches that will rise up and reclaim our cities.

## MOVING FROM HERE TO THERE

Entrepreneurial principles must be applied to reaching our communities if the church is ever to reach its full potential and obey God's calling. Doing church the same old way will only bring about the same old results. In order to affect communities for the better, pastors and their congregations are going to have to step out of the traditional mode. New wine calls for new wineskins.

And in order to transition into an entrepreneurial church, each member of the church leadership and every active member of the congregation needs to develop a personal entrepreneurial faith. This will not be easy. It will require staff leadership and laypeople alike to move out of the traditional flow and, at times, paddle against the current. It is a journey with one clear destination: to please the Lord, the original Entrepreneur.

# TEN

# FOLLOWING GOD'S ENTREPRENEURIAL SPIRIT

## God Sets the Agenda; We Get on Board

A t first glance, putting the words *entrepreneurial* and *church* in the same sentence may seem misguided and ill-advised. At its worst, the idea of entrepreneurship stirs our minds with images of money-hungry, sometimes fraudulent, wheeler-dealers who live for nothing but the bottom line. Shouldn't churches be devoted to serving faithfully, preaching the gospel, administering the sacraments, and caring for the saints? Our agenda is very different from that of the business world, so why even bother talking about entrepreneurship?

Here's why. A close look at the biblical witness reveals that the church's mission is far more than simply serving, preaching, administering the sacraments, and making sure the saints are cared for. The church is responsible to answer the call of God, which we have seen in the book of Acts is distinctly entrepreneurial. The apostle Paul caught that vision, and we see him acting entrepreneurially in at least two respects. We know he made tents to earn money that supported his missionary journeys. And more importantly, Paul found bold and innovative means to engage his culture with the gospel. With meager resources, he started new mission ventures in every port. It is estimated that within a ten-year period Paul covered more than 8,100 miles on three great missionary expeditions, which was remarkable in a day without planes, trains, or automobiles. Paul launched churches throughout the Roman world, in places like Antioch, Seleucia, Cyprus, Pamphylia, Pisidia, and Lycaonia (see Acts 13 and 14), and then on to Macedonia, Thessalonica, Berea, Athens, Corinth, Ephesus, Galatia, and Rome.[1] He and his partners would have extended their journeys into Asia, but changed their plans when the Holy Spirit prohibited them from going there (see Acts 16:6-7).

In his missionary work, Paul networked with key leaders and empowered teams to carry forth his vision. He tenaciously led others toward the goal of preaching grace and salvation to the world. And with great integrity, he passionately committed himself to the mission of the gospel. Paul made use of any resource—no matter how small—and took advantage of every opportunity to advance the Kingdom of God. This is entrepreneurship at its best! From the first century onward, entrepreneurial faith has been the vehicle that has transported the gospel around the world.

## JESUS'S FIRST ENTREPRENEURIAL FOLLOWERS

We see entrepreneurial faith exemplified even before the first Christian church was established. You remember the disciples' staring into the sky as they watched Jesus ascend to His Father? They stood there, mouths agape, not knowing what to do. Their Master, their Guide, their Leader had just left them. Suddenly, two men in white came to them.

"What are you standing around for?" asked one of the men. "Didn't Jesus just tell you to go forth and make disciples?"

"Yes, but now He's gone," said one of Jesus's followers—maybe Peter.

"And we don't know how to carry out His commission. Oh, sure, we know how the Pharisees run their meetings and recruit disciples. But I don't think Jesus wants us to do things the old way. He told us not to put new wine into old skins. It was His way of saying that if we always do what we've always done, we'll always get what we've always got."

"He taught you well. But did He not also tell you that you would not be left alone? Don't you remember His saying that He would send the Helper to be with you?"

"That sounds great," Jesus's followers said. "Tell us about this Helper."

The men in white said, "Don't you remember? Jesus said, 'It is the Holy Spirit. Stay here in Jerusalem, and He will find you'" (see Acts 1:4-5,7-11). And, of course, the Holy Sprit did find them. And after the Helper sent by the Father overwhelmed the disciples with His presence, things started happening.

Think about the amazing changes that took place in the ministry of these men after the Holy Spirit fell on them. Peter was the impulsive disciple who had proclaimed steadfast loyalty to Jesus only to later betray Him in the palace courtyard of the high priest Caiaphas (see Matthew 26:33-35, 69-74). Then this same unreliable coward, after receiving the Holy Spirit, suddenly took a great risk, both to his personal freedom and to his pride. Peter stood up in front of a crowd that just a few weeks earlier had called for the death of Jesus, and he proclaimed the divinity of Jesus. Peter took a bold initiative, this time wisely and courageously, by stepping outside the way he usually did things. And the results were amazing. Thousands were converted, and the church got its start that day in Jerusalem (see Acts 2:14-41). It had very little to do with Peter's skills and abilities and everything to do with the Holy Spirit.

The history of the early church is saturated with Holy Spirit moments. The widows and orphans felt neglected. The leaders of the church knew something should be done, but they felt their place was in teaching and proclaiming God's Word. Someone had an idea. *How about establishing a new position with a new job description—someone to look after the affairs of the needy while we continue to take care of teaching?* So a new office was created, what we now call deacons (see Acts 6:1-6). The office of deacon comprises men and women who are skilled in certain areas, such as administration, maintenance, bookkeeping, housekeeping, and the like. It took entrepreneurial thinking in the first century—thinking born in the heart of the Holy Spirit—to meets the needs of the many widows and orphans.

Then came the matter of money—not for the church or its leaders, but for new followers of Jesus. Many converts were ostracized by their families. They were evicted from their homes, they lost their jobs—all on account of their confession that Jesus was the Christ, the Son of God. There were many hungry bellies in that church.

Again, the Holy Spirit gave one or more of the leaders an idea: Let's all pool our money. This had to be a God-idea, because no one in his right mind would suggest to a group of people that those who had means should voluntarily give away their money to be used for those who were without. Why should people who worked hard, spent wisely, and saved diligently for the future now turn around and lay their money at the feet of these men, who not so long ago were poor fishermen themselves? But that is just what happened. God blessed everyone—the needy had their needs met, and the givers received more than they gave (see Acts 4:32-35). Again, an entrepreneurial idea was devised to meet a challenge.

When you read the New Testament, look for entrepreneurial faith in action. And in each case, notice that the Holy Spirit is the instigator of the idea. The Holy Spirit continues to inspire those who are willing to submit to God's plan, which, of course, is far greater than any plan we can come up with.

## Do You Fit the Description?

An entrepreneur is any individual—or any organization—committed to innovating, seizing new opportunities, and leading others to maximize the opportunities that are presented. And as we just saw, an entrepreneurial

Christian or entrepreneurial church is one that is submitted to the guidance of the Holy Spirit, inspired by the Spirit to seize opportunities, to preach the gospel boldly, and to formulate innovative approaches to meet the needs of people around them. Like the apostle Paul, effective entrepreneurial leaders draw upon imagination, commitment, passion, tenacity, integrity, teamwork, and vision to fulfill a dream.

Congregations—both new and established—are stepping forward to launch new ministries and mission-motivated enterprises that are bridging the gospel to their communities. Entrepreneurial churches and their leaders search for and seize new opportunities to share Jesus Christ with broken people. They don't limit themselves to the path of least resistance. They won't tolerate maintaining the status quo. Instead, they dream and innovate and risk for the sake of God's mission in the world.

## THE MARKS OF AN ENTREPRENEURIAL CHURCH

In our rapidly changing world, the old style of leadership is not working. Those individuals and organizations who are making a difference are practicing entrepreneurship. Four driving forces distinguish their ministries from others, and those forces can guide an effective entrepreneurial process in any part of the country, with any size church or group, and with any level of financial resources (or lack of resources).

- *The entrepreneurial church is opportunity driven.* We can imagine any number of great ideas, but which of these ideas are truly great opportunities? There's a big difference. Only 1 to 3 percent of "good ideas" translate into real projects. For an idea or opportunity to warrant action, it must be something the people want or need. Try to convince people they have a need that they don't recognize and see how far you get. The next time your committee brainstorms a number of new ideas, ask the simple question: "Which of these great ideas are also great opportunities?"

- *The entrepreneurial church is driven by a lead entrepreneur and a team.* You must ask and answer two crucial questions: Who will take the risk to lead this new venture or ministry? And who are the champions who will surround the leader? It is patently untrue that one person can lead a church to healthy growth. It takes an entrepreneurial *team* to break through the ceiling of growth. One entrepreneur can start something great, but a team of entrepreneurs can expand the dream into a powerful mission.

- *The entrepreneurial church is driven by creativity and stingy with financial resources.* It's a lie that abundant resources will necessarily lead to success. Entrepreneurs spend imagination before they spend money. Imagination goes far in producing results with very little resources. In fact, having too many resources available before the team is in place can lead to wasted resources and lost opportunities. Limited resources and stingy spending can help your organization become "lean and mean," as well as more creative. When Community Church of Joy began construction on our new campus in Phoenix, we had no money to clear the 127-acre orange grove we had purchased. A member of our staff negotiated a deal with the company building the adjacent freeway to park their trucks on our campus during road construction. In turn, they cleared the trees, saving us $250,000!

- *The entrepreneurial church is dependent on the fit and balance among these driving forces.* Entrepreneurial church leaders discern the difference between an idea and an opportunity until a new dream is born. Then they gather champions around the new dream, champions with the right mix of talents and passion for the dream. With a dream and a team, they take the appropriate risks to move forward, trusting that for everything God decides, God will provide.

# ELEVEN

# LIVING ON THE ENTREPRENEURIAL FRONTIER

## Faith Entrepreneurs Are Creative, Competent, Compassionate, Courageous

f you're an entrepreneur, you're familiar with the statement "it will never work." These are four of the most frustrating words in the English language, but they are also four of the very best words you could hear.

Think we're crazy? Think again. When someone challenges an idea or initiative based on the belief that it has no chance for success, they are actually separating human ideas from God's ideas. With God, all things are possible—even unrealistic dreams (see Matthew 19:26; Mark 10:27).

Pete Greig was the youth pastor at Revelation Church in Chichester, England. This congregation has become well known for not being your normal, everyday church. Greig and some teenagers from his church visited Herrnhutt, Germany, home of Count Nicholas von Zinzendorf, who in 1722 started a prayer meeting that continued nonstop, twenty-four hours a day, for more than one hundred years. That prayer effort began the Moravian revival, which resulted in thousands of missionaries and evangelists having an impact in Asia, North America, Africa, and Europe. In fact, Moravians made an impact on a young John Wesley during his first missions trip to America.

Inspired by the visit, Greig challenged the youth at his church to pray twenty-four hours a day for one month. "It will never work" was the expected response from others in the church. The naysayers had a rationale: *No one will want to pray in the middle of the night, and besides, if they did they would be too tired to do other work for the church.* But the church leaders eventually agreed to give it a try, setting aside a room where Greig and his young people could pray.

"The thing went absolutely crazy," says Greig.[1] "People who have hardly prayed in their lives were staying up all night. People came to the room just to sit because they could sense the presence of God."

Many people came to pray who didn't attend Revelation Church. Non-Christians came just to be there, to experience something unusual happening. Artistic gifts came forth as people turned their prayers into poems and songs, and the room filled up with paintings and drawings. God heard the prayers of these young entrepreneurs of the spirit. And, as usually happens, those who were praying felt the hand of God in their lives in ways they could never have imagined. Those who had come to this set-aside room to pray did not want it to end.

The prayer meeting was begun in September 1999. Not only did the 24-7 prayer last through that first month, it has not yet ended. There are now 24-7 Prayer Rooms in forty-five countries, with venues as diverse as the U.S. Naval Academy and a German punk music festival. The Web site set up to aid in this phenomenon, www.24-7prayer.com, is visited more than one million times a month. Outreaches to the homeless, to addicts, to those previously thought unreachable have been launched worldwide through the prayers of teenagers and adults who go in the middle of the night to a prayer room and seek the face of God. Believers young and old are seeing how God responds when His people pray.[2] This is entrepreneurial faith in action.

## THE REVERSE CONFESSION BOOTH

Reed College in Portland, Oregon, has been called the most unchristian college in America. It is a private school with a traditional semester-ending celebration called Ren Fayre. Don Miller, in his amazing book *Blue Like Jazz,* describes Ren Fayre as an alcohol and drug fest deluxe. Nudity is the preferred dress code. A beer garden is set up where kegs are seemingly in limitless supply. In anticipation of students falling as casualties to the hedonism, college officials enlist the services of Whitebird, a medical unit that specializes in helping people through bad trips and drug overdoses. Ren Fayre is not where you want to go for your next family vacation.

But it is precisely where Don Miller and the few Christians who attend Reed College decided they wanted to "come out of the closet." They had been told that Christians could never have a positive impact at Reed. Churches in the Portland area warned young people to stay away from Reed. So it was with great trepidation that Don and his friends moved forward with their plan.

They set up a confessional booth on campus during Ren Fayre. They built it out of plywood and two-by-fours and painted "Confessional" over the doorway. The interior was sectioned off with a curtain so one person would sit on one side, with Miller or one of his friends on the other side. But here was the catch: Miller did not *take* confessions from the partygoers. Miller and the other Christians were the ones who *did the confessing.* They confessed how they had been judgmental rather than loving toward the other students at Reed. They confessed how they had not done enough to care for the poor and hungry. They confessed that they had failed to faithfully represent Jesus on campus.

The reaction to this reverse confessional was overwhelming. The effects lasted long after the drinking at Ren Fayre was nothing but a bad headache. Many students who had been vehemently opposed to Christianity now paused to listen to the believers on campus. Weekly trips to serve at a homeless shelter in Portland resulted in turning away students because the van was always full. Four Bible studies started for those who were not believers but wanted to know more about Jesus.[3] This is entrepreneurial faith in action.

It took courage and boldness—some might even say lunacy—for Christians to confess their sins to a random procession of drunken, lewd, pleasure-seeking college students. But Don Miller and his fellow believers felt the leading of God to do just that. It made a lasting impact, but making the transition from ministry-as-usual to bold ministry that strays far from the sanctuary is no easy process.

Too many churches and Christian ministries are, to put it bluntly, boring. We have been entrusted with the most amazing, compelling, and needed story in the world—the story of God's limitless love for us. Yet we won't bother to develop a fresh, creative way to present that story to those who are dying to hear it. Stop and think about the incredible gospel story. God came to our world, in human form, to perform the greatest search-and-rescue mission of all time. The gospel might seem unreasonable or unrealistic or too simple or raise any number of other objections from those who hear it. But we can never say that it's boring. God, the Creator of the universe, is not boring. Boredom should be banned from all churches and from the life of every Christian!

The most creative person the world has ever seen is Jesus Christ. You don't get a lot more creative than turning water into wine. And that was just His first miracle. One of the last things He did on earth was to walk into a room through a closed door. If that's not creative, nothing is.

If we profess that "it is no longer I who live, but Christ lives in me" (Galatians 2:20, NASB; see also Ephesians 3:17, 4:13), then we have the Creator living in us and through us. So why do we settle for doing the same boring things, saying the same things in the same boring way, maintaining boring programs that long ago lost their sense of mission?

There is only one group that can tolerate this level of boredom—those who wish to keep the status quo. They will listen to boring sermons, sing hymns that sound like dirges, pray rote prayers using the same words and the same intonation that they have been repeating for years. They would never admit that their church's biggest attraction is that it's boring, but they acknowledge it using other words. "We once tried to change things around, and it didn't work. In fact, it was a disaster!" These people draw boundaries around their churches to keep the Holy Spirit, whose job it is to initiate change in our hearts, on the outside. When God is locked out of the church, it's guaranteed to be boring inside.

But consider how exciting things become when the Ultimate Entrepreneur is active within us. Our creativity explodes. We are no longer bound by tradition or limited by conventional boundaries. Whatever we have learned—be it in seminary, in church, on the job, in relationships—that has put you in a box, that box suddenly gets torn apart. We have the mind of Christ, and His mind is never contained by a box.

Boring churches are populated by boring Christians, people who are content to stay where they have always been. You may be a pastor of a boring church, or you may be a member of one. In either case, when you unleash entrepreneurial faith, you make a difference. You can knock down false limitations and participate in the "new thing" that God is doing today. I guarantee you it is much more fun than anchoring a pew in a boring church.

## Reject Boredom

If you are ready to leave boring church life behind in exchange for the risky life of the Spirit, then think through the following core principles that undergird every pursuit of entrepreneurial faith. Moving a congregation or any group of Christians from secure and boring to risky, outward-focused, and creative is a matter of following these guiding principles, each beginning with the letter C as an aid to memory.

## Creativity

Entrepreneurs are creative. Here is another definition of an entrepreneur: *Someone who assumes responsibility and takes the risk of starting a new venture.* Starting from scratch, bringing something into being where there was nothing before, demands a creative mindset—seeing what needs to be, but doesn't yet exist, and bringing it into being. Creativity is not just artistic expression, although that certainly can be a part of entrepreneurial faith. Creative thinking involves seeing through the eyes of God, believing that He can do what seems impossible, and courageously acting on what you see and believe. Remember, the Spirit of God is seldom safe, and He is never boring.

## Competency

Not only must entrepreneurs be creative, but they must also be competent. Mediocrity will not cut it in the business world, so why do we accept it in the world of Christian faith? Where are the believers who strive for excellence in everything that concerns the gospel message? The business world knows the difference between well done and poorly done. It's time for the church to go and do likewise.

This is not to say that we should attempt to out-entertain the world. Many consider the Rolling Stones to be the greatest entertainers, at least in the world of rock music. Commanding astounding ticket prices and selling out huge concert venues allows them to use high-tech visual effects, along with pyrotechnics and an incredible sound system for their shows. There's no way a church service, or even a Christian concert, can compete with this level of technical excellence in entertainment. But the *message* we have to share, unlike that of the Rolling Stones, is one that is worth listening to.

## Compassion

Creative and competent believers must also be compassionate. Love, said the apostle Paul, is the greatest character trait of all (see 1 Corinthians 13:13). You can develop the greatest entrepreneurial ministry in the nation, but if you don't love those in your neighborhood and in your town or city, you are singing a silent tune. Compassion for others is what marks us as followers of Jesus. "Love each other…," said Jesus. "Your love for one another will prove to the world that you are my disciples" (John 13:34-35). As entrepreneurs, it can be easy to get wrapped up in our plans, selling the vision and burning with passion to move forward—while we forget the most important thing: to love the people God has called us to reach.

## Courage

The first three principles that guide entrepreneurial ministry will never move things beyond an idea, discussion, prayer, and planning without the final ingredient: courage. Just as God's call in our lives is never boring, neither is it safe. If we lack courage, we will shy away from the risks involved in meeting the needs of our communities. Queen Esther risked her very life in approaching the king without his bidding—which in ancient times was a capital offense. But she took the risk because a new decree had been issued to destroy all the Jews living in the empire of King Xerxes. The queen protected her people by appealing to the king, but not without putting her own life on the line. As we have seen in the book of Acts, the Holy Spirit gives us power and boldness so we can overcome our timidity and our attachment to comfort and safety. We need courage if we're to translate God's vision into reality.

## THE FOUR CS IN ACTION

Think about the story of four first-century entrepreneurs who took their hurting friend to see Jesus (see Mark 2:1-12). The friend was paralyzed, so the men had to carry him on a stretcher. By the time they arrived, the house where Jesus was speaking was packed. The men climbed a ladder onto the roof, taking their friend along on the stretcher. That was creative. Then they demonstrated their competence, opening a hole in the roof wide enough to lower their friend down to Jesus. They opened the roof at just the right place, so that they didn't bring the house crashing down on those inside. Obviously, they had compassion for their friend. Why else would they go to all this trouble? And from the start, the four men acted with courage. They exposed themselves to the likelihood of ridicule, and they damaged the roof of a home without knowing how the homeowner would react. And besides, they went to all this trouble without knowing for certain that Jesus would have time to heal the paralyzed friend. From start to finish, our four C principles guided their vision, passion, and actions. They were determined to do whatever it took to help their friend walk again.

If the church is to see the paralyzed in our communities walk again, it must become entrepreneurial. In the near future, it will become a matter of survival. Churches that refuse to become entrepreneurial by reaching beyond the sanctuary walls with the gospel will simply fade away. If you don't believe us, look back at this book's introduction to see what is happening with millions of eighteen- to twenty-nine-year-olds in America. They are the most religiously disaffected generation ever to live in this country. So let us all start being entrepreneurial with the gospel. Either that, or prepare to see our churches disappear.

# PART III

# GOD'S VISION FOR THE ENTREPRENEUR

# TWELVE

# EARTHBOUND IDEA OR GOD'S VISION?

## Separating the Dreams from the Schemes

One of the wisest men ever to live proclaimed, "Where there is no vision, the people perish" (Proverbs 29:18, KJV). Two things that set spiritual entrepreneurs apart from others are that God gives them a vision and they are able to recognize it as coming from God. Part of seeing God's vision is developing an attitude of expectation when facing a need or a challenge. This is a constant attitude of dreaming of new ways to shine a light in the darkness. It's a heart-driven desire to find new and effective ways to rescue your hurting neighbors.

Entrepreneurial faith comes from the Holy Spirit. In order to endure the hardships, long hours, numerous setbacks and, oftentimes, ridicule that accompany being an entrepreneur for the gospel, you must know with confidence that your vision is from God. If you don't cling to this knowledge, you may find it too tempting to give up. To exercise the entrepreneurial faith that accomplishes what God is calling you to do, you must follow the Spirit. And we believe that all lasting visions come from God. We agree with Martin Luther's interpretation of the third article of the Apostles' Creed:

> I believe that I cannot by my own reason or strength believe in Jesus Christ or come to him, but that the Holy Spirit has called me through the Gospel, enlightened me with gifts, and sanctified and preserved me in the one true faith.

Walking in the Spirit with entrepreneurial faith requires that you have clear vision to see what God wants you to see, faith to believe what God shows you, and courage to act on what you see. These three—vision, faith, and courage to act—are separate, but they work together. In this section, we will help you check your vision.

## WITHOUT A VISION...

God created us with the need for a driving force in our lives. We long for a foe to conquer, a cause to champion, a challenge that will take our very best to overcome. Christian author John Eldredge says we were made to be "wild at heart."[1] Without this drive—call it a vision, a dream, a burning desire— we sit still and do nothing, accomplish nothing, become nothing. Without a vision, we wither up inside, having no reason to exist.

When we speak of vision, we are not necessarily referring to a vision in the prophetic sense or one that appears in a miraculous way. Although for some, that is how the dream starts. But for most, having vision means that we see ourselves, our mission, and the world around us as God sees these things. On our own, we have very limited vision. And we don't get much because we don't see much.

God told Abram to look around him. "Look north, south, east, and west," said God. "I am going to give it all to you and your children. Your family tree will spread far and wide and will last forever" (see Genesis 13:14-16). God gave this ancient man of faith a vision!

Most of us only see what's right in front of us, so that's all we understand. It's all we can grasp. And it's as far as our human nature can take us. Our restricted vision limits our usefulness to the cause of the Kingdom. We need to lift up our eyes and look beyond our current situation. It's impossible to pursue and accomplish what we cannot see.

In Numbers 13–14 we read that Joshua and Caleb came back from spying out the land of Canaan. They reported the incredible opportunities across the river. But the others who went with them had limited vision. They only saw the giants that were standing in their way. We need to have the vision of Joshua and Caleb, who looked beyond the giant obstacles and saw the giant opportunities God had set before them.

A God-breathed vision is what keeps you pumped up—or "geeked" as the young people say. It may be a simple idea that makes a small adjustment to an existing program, or it may be a dream so outrageous that it appears impossible. But if this idea burns in your heart day and night, and it is consistent with Scripture, it is most likely from God. Those who develop entrepreneurial faith, who are always looking for mountains to climb, who are never satisfied with "good enough," will come to rely on God-given visions as much as their natural sight.

But as we begin to talk about vision, realize the great difference between a dream and a scheme. Dreams lead to new ways to give help to the poor and hurting people around you. Dreams fulfilled will leave you feeling great inside, even though you have expended much time and energy to bring the vision to reality. Schemes, on the other hand, may appear to be aimed at helping others, but they really benefit only a few while taking a great deal from a great many. Schemes drain some people to add unfairly to others. Schemes may make you wealthy but will never make you rich in God and His grace. Dreams, on the other hand, advance the Kingdom of God. That is, when we pursue the dreams that God gives so they can become reality.

## The Danger of a Vision

Dreams and visions, like entrepreneurial faith itself, are risky ventures. No one said this was safe or easy. Remember that when God puts a vision in your heart and you set out to make it a reality, you are going to face opposition. And it will come in ways you never expected.

When I (Walt) first came to Community Church of Joy, the vision statement for the church was pretty much the same as for most denominational churches at that time. The church wanted to set an atmosphere that would attract those new to the community who had been raised in a Lutheran church. The vision statement, had it been written out, would have read something like this:

> We want to be open to all those of Lutheran upbringing who move into our community. We will honor the longtime traditions of the Lutheran church in order to attract those Lutherans looking for a Lutheran church.

Christians who move to a new city do, in fact, need to find a church home in their new location. But this vision statement had major problems, and the size of the problem became clear as I surveyed the surrounding community. There were many unchurched people living within a convenient drive to our location, but few—if any—were Lutherans. They had never been Lutheran. As a matter of fact, most of them were not Christian. These people did not have a church tradition as part of their upbringing. That meant that our church's approach—offering a traditional Lutheran liturgical service—had no appeal to these neighbors. If we wanted to reach our community and grow our church, we had to find a new vision.

When Community Church of Joy moved to our new campus in 1998, we restated our vision as a mission to reach the unchurched. We made this vision clear to the congregation. We built our campus with this purpose in mind. It was designed to look more like a shopping mall than a traditional church. We started a K-8 school to serve the needs of the community. We made the facility available to nonmembers for community use. Within a few months, the church campus was used for meetings of our local Chamber of Commerce, American Express corporate banquets, high-school awards ceremonies, and student assemblies. One local school used it for their prom. Two of the teens walked around our campus, picked up a brochure, and decided to visit one of our services. They then began attending our church. Local recovery groups found that the facilities met their needs as well. We were really starting to reach the community.

We were surprised when some staff members and longtime attendees voiced their displeasure over our vision. They felt their needs were being overlooked for the sake of outreach. They felt minimized. Didn't we know that they had needs too? One member commented, "I'm tired of hearing about the unchurched! Let's take care of our own people first. These outsiders leave a mess, and we have to clean up after them. Shouldn't you first take care of us who pay the bills?"

These people had not thought through the personal sacrifices they would have to make nor the changes they would have to endure, such as changing the familiar meeting times and places, lack of space, exhaustion of the cleanup crews, and strain on the budget. Thousands of people left us. Yes, thousands. And I'm not speaking figuratively. That's when we found out just how costly it can be to follow your vision. If we had been looking at things through human eyes, we would have started calculating how much money those thousands had been giving and how much revenue we were losing every Sunday. And remember that this was occurring just as we were occupying a new campus with higher utility bills, higher insurance premiums, and greater staff needs. At a time like that, it's important to be sure that what you are following is a dream from God, not a scheme from within yourself.

## A HUMAN SCHEME OR GOD'S VISION FOR YOU?

How can you tell if what is in your heart is a dream or a scheme? Sometimes, at least at the beginning, it can be hard to tell them apart. Here are six characteristics of a godly vision from Kirbyjon:

- *A vision leads to helping others.* If you have a desire to improve upon a product or service, and the end result will be a benefit to others, this could be the real deal. On the other hand, if your dream is for your own personal advancement or gain, check again. You've probably landed on a scheme.

- *A vision glorifies God.* Who gets the credit when the vision is fulfilled? Will your name be on the flag that flies over the finished product, or will it be the name of the One who enabled you to complete it? If you are looking forward to more appearances on the speaking circuit and a book-signing tour following the completion of the project, you may be hooked to a scheme rather than a dream.

- *A vision is future oriented.* A divine vision brings confidence in the future, no matter how little of it has yet materialized. Just because it hasn't happened doesn't mean it will not happen. It may call for resources or skills you don't yet have. Visions must be *built,* as opposed to simply unwrapped. If what you are proposing already exists, you are simply moving one person's fulfilled vision onto your property. That's not a divine vision. Wait on God for futuristic visions.

- *A vision defeats the work of the devil.* Jesus said He came to destroy the works of the devil. If we are working side by side with Jesus, we will be doing the same. Our vision will lead to destruction of the schemes constructed by Satan. We often have to demolish old structures before we can build new ones. God breaks through the devil's schemes of self-centeredness, ego, and apathy toward a broken world so that Jesus's love can shine through.

- *A vision requires the power of the Holy Spirit.* If we can bring the dream to pass on our own, without God's help, it is simply a scheme. It's too small and too earthbound to qualify as a vision. Real visions given by God require God's power, expressed in our lives through the Holy Spirit, to be completed. This is why all of the credit for bringing a vision to reality goes to God.

- *A vision advances God's Kingdom.* After all, that is what we are to be about. If our thoughts and actions are not advancing God's perfect way, they are schemes. On the other hand, when our visions and dreams line up with Scripture, and they promote the Kingdom of God, we can move ahead with unshakable confidence.

Is it a dream or a scheme? Make absolutely sure before moving ahead.

# THIRTEEN

# KEEPING OPPONENTS AT BAY

## Guarding the Vision While Hearing the Real Truth

**M**ovies with sword fights are great entertainment, especially when the heroine has to fight two villains at once. She has to hop around, constantly turning, swinging her sword in front and behind, since she is outnumbered. To ward off the enemies, she has to defend against blows from all sides. Yeah, movies are great.

But what happens when you feel like you're the person in a sword fight, and you're not battling just two opponents? You're being attacked by a small army. If you're practicing entrepreneurial faith, that's likely to happen. In fact, if you're encountering absolutely no opposition, you're doing something wrong. If God gave you a vision, and you are faithfully pursuing the vision, then you have entered a spiritual battle. An attack could come from any quarter, or all quarters at the same time. Get ready.

Before we get to a discussion of the serious enemies who want to destroy God's vision and prevent His work from being done, let's look first at the ordinary people who may oppose your vision not out of evil motives but simply because they fear change. This is the natural reaction whenever a new approach is suggested. And entrepreneurs can be so passionate about a vision that those who are just now being informed of the plan can easily feel left out, out of touch, and even left behind.

There is a way the entrepreneurial leader, whether pastor or committee chair or ministry director, can win those opponents over as allies—or at least as neutral bystanders.

## Winning the Easy Battle

We call this the "easy" battle not because it's an easy one to win, but because it's not a war against spiritual enemies. Instead, it's a challenge that requires wise leadership, good communication skills, and a patient and tactful process of helping others buy into your vision. Don't let your excitement scare off those who might well join you but first need to become familiar with the dream before they'll commit.

Here are three ways an entrepreneur of faith can enlist allies to the cause of pursuing God's vision.

### Persuade; Don't Badger

People are inherently averse to change, even when a change will improve their lives or, in this case, will lead to new and needed ministries that will touch lives with the gospel of grace. Any new approach will be uncomfortable to some and threatening to others. So to avoid unnecessary opposition, bring the congregation, church board, or committee members along gradually. Don't frighten them with your enthusiasm. After all, you've been cooking on this vision for some time, and they are just now becoming aware of it. So be patient as you present what you have heard from God. A little patience and care in introducing the vision will go a long way toward winning over those who are initially reluctant or even opposed to the change. And remember, badgering never won over an opponent. So the canings must stop!

## Assume the Best

When someone is critical of your vision, don't automatically assume that the person is an enemy. He or she might simply be saying, without actually saying it, that more information is needed. So begin with the assumption that people are with you, that they're for you, and that they want to do the right thing. When you communicate your passion for the vision, be positive in motivating others. Tell stories that connect the people with the mission you see in your vision. If certain things have already been set into motion, celebrate small victories along the way. And be sure to credit the heroes. People are interested in people. What else could explain the popularity of reality shows on television? So use that natural interest to present the vision in the context of helping people who have real needs—key in on the human-interest angle. And don't forget humor. A little laughter can ease the tension among people who are anxious over the unknown arriving right at their doorstep.

## Neutralize Opposition

After your best efforts to bring others on board, you will find that some prefer to remain on the sidelines. Or worse, some will be heading over to join the opponents' camp. Still, this does not mean they are committed enemies. At least not yet. They may simply be people with hurt feelings, or those who aren't yet willing to trade security and comfort for risk and adventure. Even if they won't ever get on board, you can take steps to prevent them from taking up arms against you.

An important step in this regard is to understand that just because God gave you this vision, it's not necessarily a vision for everyone around you. So gently invite those who are on the sidelines to either agree to remain neutral or to graciously leave. No leader likes to encourage an exodus, but people who aren't following are not followers, even if they stick around.

## ENEMIES BENT ON DESTRUCTION

We now move from the easy battle to the war that has eternal stakes. The constant opponent who remains in front of you is *the* Enemy—Satan. He goes all-out to try to stop any advancement of the Kingdom of God. As we saw in the previous chapter, God gives us visions so that His Kingdom can be made more visible on earth. So be prepared for attacks from the Evil One. Be sure to daily put on the armor of God (see Ephesians 6:12-17). Sharpen your sword by reading, memorizing, and studying Scripture. The breastplate of righteousness (God's righteousness, not yours) and the helmet of salvation are there to protect your two most vulnerable areas—your heart and your head. Wear shoes of peace, so everywhere you walk you will leave God-inspired footprints for others to follow. And don't forget your shield of faith.

The late Tom Skinner, a great African American preacher who rose out of the Harlem street gangs to become, among other things, the chaplain for the Washington Redskins, used to say that Christians have no problem putting on the armor of God. We like wearing the armor. It's just that once we get it all on, we're afraid to face the devil. But since we already have the armor on, we don't want to waste it. So we fight each other.

Satan's opposition to God's vision is guaranteed, but there is a second front on which you may need to fight. That's the fight among your fellow believers. Divine visions shake up the status quo. And when things start shaking, people start complaining. Some of these complaints will turn to criticism, and some of the criticism can turn ugly. Some in the church may be mean-spirited enough to make their attacks personal, and others will resort to half-truths and outright lies. That's why you can't be a true entrepreneurial leader if you have a low emotional quotient. By this we mean if you can't stand the heat of rejection and ridicule, don't come into the kitchen where new, untested ideas are baking!

If you are too wounded by such attacks, ask God whether you are better suited to a number two spot on the team, serving alongside another entrepreneurial leader. Perhaps your gifts are better exercised on the team as administrator—keeping logistics and details straight, organizing the troops. Or you might be gifted to be the finance person, the recruiter of talent, the networker to get others in the community involved, or to serve in some other capacity. If you're not emotionally resilient, don't attempt to be the point person. It will destroy you.

## DON'T GIVE IN, AND DON'T GIVE UP

You know the toll that warfare takes. Some of your supporters will drop out of the fight and then drop out of sight. Former allies can simply disappear. A few of your supporters might even shift allegiances, joining the opposition and breaking trust with you.

Then there's the internal war. Satan will try to steal your peace. Opponents in the community will use public forums to try to shift public opinion against your initiatives. Some will misrepresent your words or your plans or your intentions. Faultfinders in your church will organize clandestine pockets of negativity. Some will demand that you give an accounting for your "harebrained schemes."

People will question your ability to hear from God: "And just why do you think you can hear God's voice? Do you have a special connection that we don't have? Why didn't God tell the rest of us what He's telling you?"

In the heat of battle, it's easy for all the opposition, the wearying fight, and the continued demands of having to fulfill ordinary duties in addition to launching new initiatives to make you feel like giving up. Why keep struggling to do something that no one seems to support? Maybe you really are confused about hearing from God. It's all just too tiring to keep up the fight to move forward.

Isn't it?

Yes and no. Yes, it *is* exhausting—both physically and spiritually. And no, don't let your enemies kill your vision. God gave you a vision for a reason. And it's not primarily for your good. It's not designed to make you feel that you're contributing something significant to help your community. It's for the good of those who need to hear from God, in the gospel message, and to feel God's touch in the form of tangible help—through ministries of mercy in your locality. So refuse to let go, no matter what the naysayers do or say.

## How to Defeat the Vision Killers

As a relatively older dad with three young children, I (Kirbyjon) am persuaded that visions are like newborn infants. They are fragile and susceptible to injury, to disease, and to those who would treat them with disdain. You must protect your vision, just as you would protect a newborn. And knowing what you are protecting the vision *from* is helpful. Here are three vision killers that can attack and destroy the divine dream you are pursuing.

### The Spirit of "I Am a Success"

Studies have shown that organizations are most likely to make a deadly decision just when they are experiencing success. Optimal decisions are not made when you are soaring with the eagles. Most mountain-climbing accidents happen on the way down the slope, after the exhilaration of having reached the summit.

A new vision keeps you from becoming complacent with the way things are. It keeps you reaching beyond what you can easily grasp. It's the struggle of moving forward when the path is rocky that keeps you sharp and relying on God. So be thankful that God continues to pour new visions into your heart. This is what keeps you humble as you move ahead.

## The Spirit of "I Can Explain"

When problems arise—and they will—do you try to explain away the problem? If so, you are in denial—and denial is the opposite of living in the truth. You're lying about circumstances and challenges, and you don't even know it. Mostly, you're lying to yourself. If you explain away problems, it is a step toward the death of your vision.

A real entrepreneur understands that excuses are counterproductive. Excuses accomplish nothing, and they stand in the way of real progress. Instead of explaining away a problem, face it head-on. Admit quickly when things don't go as you planned. After all, as an entrepreneur, you do not fear trouble!

## The Spirit of "I Hear What I Want"

This mindset is your teammates telling you what they think you want to hear rather than what you need to hear. Leaders can be threatening, and telling them the truth can be hard.

Those who follow a leader tend to talk the way they think the leader wants them to talk. This is a dangerous threat to your vision. You need to be intentional in hearing what you need to hear and receiving what you need to receive. You need to, at whatever the cost, be sure you are getting the hard, cold, brutal, unvarnished facts from those around you. We tend to assemble followers who would gladly drink our bath water. Instead, be sure to surround yourself with people who will tell you the hard truth.

One restaurant owner in Houston came up with a unique way to find out what his customers like and don't like. In the past, he would wander through the dining area to ask diners how they liked their food. When the patrons found out this was the owner asking about their dinner, they would invariably say everything was just fine. But the owner knew it was impossible for everyone to love everything. So instead of asking the customers, who would readily lie to him, he went out back and looked into the trash cans. What food was being thrown away? Was there a pattern to what was *not* being eaten? From his detective work, he made adjustments to his menu that increased customer satisfaction and ultimately increased his business.

Sometimes finding the truth involves going through some garbage. You will need to launch your own method of "trash can detection." Look at the programs and services you have initiated. Perhaps when you first mentioned them, those around you told you what great ideas they were. But then after the program was launched, few people showed up to take advantage of what was being offered. You now need to look in the trash can to find out what is not being used so you can make needed adjustments.

Real entrepreneurs know how to protect the vision from every type of enemy. And as they champion the vision, they also invite the truth—even if it's sometimes hard to hear. Being faithful to carry out God's vision, and then making needed adjustments along the way, requires the truth. So make sure you demand it from those around you.

# FOURTEEN

# TOSS THE SACRED COWS ONTO THE GRILL

## How to Get Around Obstacles That Can Derail Your Vision

Beads of sweat formed on his forehead as Martin Luther stood before the king and his court. They expected him to buckle under their pressure and renounce the books he had written against the powerful religious leaders of his day. This was the moment they had all been waiting for—friends and foes alike. Would the Augustinian monk, who had rediscovered the power of faith, God's Word, and grace, fall to the power of the Pope? Would his grand vision of freedom for Christians be lost?

Finally, inspired by the Spirit of God, Luther declared:

Unless I am convinced by the teachings of Holy Scripture or by sound reasoning—for I do not believe either the pope or councils alone, since they have often made mistakes and have even said the

exact opposite about the same point—I am tied by the Scriptures
I have quoted and by my conscience. I cannot and will not recant
anything. For to go against conscience is neither safe nor right. Here
I stand. God help me! Amen.[1]

The room erupted with noise. Some were ready to kill the monk as a
heretic. Others celebrated that Luther had opened the floodgates to a new
way of living the Christian life—not under the thumb of a human authority,
but by the power of the Holy Spirit. Luther bucked the system in a huge way.

Bucking the system is not the solution to every challenge we encounter.
But bringing a vision to reality often requires an entrepreneur to see beyond the
constraints of the current systems. Luther saw beyond. You can see beyond.

Both of our ministries live within the bounds of a long tradition of faith.
For Windsor Village, it's the Methodist denomination; for the Community
Church of Joy, it's the Lutheran tradition. Both of these denominations carry
tremendous gifts of rich theology and systems that support God's mission.
These traditions are meant to serve like a ship's rudder guiding us into the
future, rather than as an anchor holding us to the past.

Yet it seems that for many churches or parachurch ministries, the traditions of the past become sacred cows that stand in the way of new vision
being birthed. Business consultants will tell you that health-care systems and
institutions of higher learning have the most stubborn corporate cultures on
the face of the earth. We would add churches to that list. The reason for this
reluctant-to-change culture is that those who run these organizations tend to
be tenured, entrenched, stubborn, and territorial.

In other words, they cling to sacred cows.

Sacred cows are systems, policies, and procedures that may have been
useful at one time, but now are past their prime. Yet no one dares touch
them. "This is how we have always done it" is the barbed-wire fence protecting these cows.

When you are ready to step out in entrepreneurial faith, know that you are going to step on some toes. You must be willing to fire up the grill and toss a few sacred cows onto it. It may be smoky for a while, but after the smoke clears, your vision will still be there. And what separates the "saints" from the "aints" as it relates to a vision is execution. As a matter of fact, one of the main causes of burnout among pastors and other leaders is that they don't execute their visions. They spend all their time and energy dancing around worn-out systems—sacred cows—and never see their vision fulfilled. After a while, they simply give up.

There are five key components to the execution of a vision. Remember, a vision is simply where you want to go. It has nothing to do with where you have been. Just because it has not been done before does not mean you can't do it. Grill the sacred cow that says, "You can't because you haven't."

## MISSION WITH PASSION

The first component to fulfilling a vision is mission. Ask yourself, "Why do I exist? What is my purpose?" Or put it this way: Of all the funerals you have been to, why is it that none has been yours? You are alive today. Why?

Finding your purpose will help you define your vision. But mission alone will not help in executing the vision. You must add passion to your purpose. Passion will help you get through the negativity, fear, and exhaustion that will come as you put your vision into place. Mission with enthusiasm will also help others who are working alongside you to get through the hard times.

Understand this. Where there is vision, there will be division. It may be around the board table or around the coffee maker. It may be in the parking lot or in the lobby. It may be official or unofficial. But it will be there. This makes mission with passion so important to the successful execution of a vision.

That sacred cow marked NO EMOTION? Toss it onto the barbecue!

## Strategies and Structures

We said there are five key components to executing a vision. The first, mission with passion, we just considered. The last, the people on your team, will get its own discussion in the following chapter. Two of the middle components—strategies and tactics, and structure—have already been written about extensively. Browse the business section of your local bookstore or library and you will find countless good books dealing with these topics.

So in this context—helping faith entrepreneurs bring about their vision—let's simply look at the meanings of these words.

The English word *stratagem* comes from the Greek *strategie,* meaning "be a general." *Strategia,* or "generalship," became our word *strategy.* These words, of course, have military underpinnings. In order to advance your vision, you must become a general—the leader of the team that will execute the vision.

The word *tactics* also comes from Greek words used to describe military actions. It refers to the small things you do in order to accomplish a larger task. Both strategy (effective leadership) and tactics (the ordering of a group of actions in order to accomplish your goal) are needed to enact your vision.

The meaning behind the word *structure* also relates directly to seeing a vision become reality. The Latin *structura* means "the process of building." What goes into the process of building your vision? Is it a physical building, such as a larger sanctuary or a Power Center in a vacant Kmart? Is it a Friday-night program formatted to attract high-school students? Is it a business that will train young entrepreneurs? Structures come in all shapes and sizes. There is no right or wrong structure—but any structure can be put to a right or wrong use. And as for strategy and tactics, there are many good resources available to help you in the process of building your vision with the best structure in mind. Let's move on to the fourth key component in executing vision.

## Can You Hear Me Now?

Business consultants refer to this fourth component as "systems," and they analyze these systems a lot. With spiritual entrepreneurship in mind, we will focus on systems of communication.

How does communication flow in your church, organization, or committee? We know the general can talk to the privates, but can the privates talk with the general? Does information flow only from top to bottom, or can it also flow from bottom to top? Is yours a system of empowerment, where everyone is involved in the execution of the vision? Or is it a system of entitlement, where you have to have been there for years in order to be heard?

Please understand this: The more archaic and vertical your system of communication is, the more difficult it will be to implement your vision. If those in your organization don't feel free to disagree with you, if the only team members you recruit are those who will gladly drink your bath water, you will not hear the truth you need. So stoke the grill and roast the sacred cow of one-way communication in your organization.

## A Wild Card

Before we move on to the fifth key component—people—in the next chapter, let's look at a wild card that will affect you. Even if you have all five essential components in place—mission with passion, strategy and tactics, structure, systems of communication, and people—there is another element you must be aware of: culture. When we talk about culture, we don't necessarily mean the society in which you live (although there are some aspects of that culture affecting the execution of your vision). We're referring instead to the culture of your organization and the people who will be affected by your vision. Cultures, just like individuals, can be stubborn and resistant to change.

When I (Kirbyjon) announced the building of Corinthian Pointe in

Houston, with plans for 454 affordable, single-family homes, the people living in the surrounding neighborhoods said, "Oh no! Slum housing!"

When they heard that the residential development would target those with low to moderate income, these neighbors automatically associated that with "slums." They could only see with their old vision. What they did not know was that a new vision was being cast that would redefine the existing culture. When they saw the first houses completed, with trees in the front yard, sidewalks, and even the house numbers painted in the same place on each house, they finally abandoned their old idea and caught our vision.

Be ready. When a vision is cast, there are a lot of nuances and dynamics in the culture that will try to destroy the vision. Beware of the sacred cows that roam in your culture. They make a lot of noise, and they look unmovable. But once you light the charcoal and the grill is ready, there's room to roast all of those cows.

Remember, sacred cows make the best barbecue!

# FIFTEEN

# FINDING THE BEST PEOPLE

## How to Attract the Ones Who Will Turn Vision into Reality

**A**s we noted earlier, without a vision the people will perish. But likewise, without the right people, the vision will perish. Having the right people around you is the fifth key component to the execution of your vision. On any given day, the people you surround yourself with can be your greatest assets or your biggest liabilities.

First, you need to stop thinking in terms of employees and begin thinking of teams. You *are* building a team, aren't you? Not just employees who report to you or volunteers who shuffle papers, but a team of passionate workers who have a common goal: to see the vision become reality.

The primary quality of any successful team is commitment to a common goal. Without this commitment, each person simply performs as an individual. But when individuals share a common commitment to the same goal, the team develops synergy—becoming much stronger than the sum of its parts. As Joe Paterno, Penn State's legendary football coach, would say, "When a team outgrows individual performance and learns team confidence, excellence becomes a reality."[1]

## PYRAMID OR FLAT LINE?

The typical organizational chart—be it of a for-profit organization, nonprofit corporation, school, or church—is shaped more or less like a pyramid. The CEO/president/pastor sits at the top, with descending levels of managers and workers making up the lower levels. In this model, the person at the top makes a decision, and the work is carried out by those at various levels below. Ideas generated by someone at the very bottom of the pyramid rarely are heard by those at the top, no matter how good the idea is.

Teamwork is more like a flat line. There is still a leader—the person with the vision—but the entire team is empowered to help execute the vision. In the typical structure, each person is individually accountable for his or her tasks. But in a team structure, each person is accountable to one another. Synergy develops, allowing the group to accomplish more than the individuals can when operating independently. In a team, anyone can share an idea—which, in turn, often sparks additional ideas.

The first step you must take as the visionary is to stop thinking like an old-fashioned boss. Instead of issuing orders to be carried out by those below you, you need to coordinate a team of thinking teammates, working together to solve problems and advance your vision. The team leader is a motivator, continually casting the vision before those who will help bring it to pass.

Some of the ways a team leader successfully leads the team include:

- clearly articulating the organization's mission;
- clearly articulating the team's mission as it relates to the overall organization;
- assuring that communication flows freely in *all* directions;
- assessing the strengths and weaknesses of each team member (the wise leader then uses the strength of each team member

while avoiding assigning him or her tasks that will play to his or her weaknesses); and

- continually motivating the team to keep moving toward their goal, especially through the inevitable tough times.

## GOOFUS OR GALLANT?

You do not have a team if you are still looking over every shoulder, approving every purchase order, editing every memo, and dissecting every discussion. Team leaders are not micromanagers—they must learn to let go, even knowing that mistakes will be made. If your teammates are not given the latitude to make mistakes, they will never accomplish great things.

Remember the characters Goofus and Gallant, two very opposite boys in the old *Highlights* magazines you read at the doctor's office when you were young? Think of Goofus as a traditional boss and Gallant as an enlightened team leader.

- Goofus tells his employees: "Do this." Gallant says: "Let's work on this together."
- Goofus threatens. Gallant encourages.
- Goofus thinks work should be hard. Gallant thinks work should be fun.
- Goofus says: "Do it because I'm the boss and I said so." Gallant says: "Perhaps there is a better way to do this. Do you have any ideas?"
- Goofus says: "That's not the way we do it here." Gallant says: "I never would have thought of that. Great job!"
- Teams are led by Gallant, not Goofus. So don't be a Goofus.

## DO YOU WANT THREES OR EIGHTS FOLLOWING YOU?

One of the most common complaints we hear from pastors and business leaders is the inability to hire and retain a great staff. This problem goes far beyond offering comparable pay and a fun environment to work in. The problem is not with the staff. The problem is with the leader.

Wait! Don't stop reading yet. Hear us out.

Before you point your finger at "disloyal" staff members, take a good look in the mirror. On a scale of ten, where do you land as a leader? If you are a six, be assured that an eight is not going to follow you, at least not for very long. Threes will follow you, but there is only so much a three can give you. Before you try to staff your team with eights, nines, and tens, you may have to work to raise your own level on the scale.

Not everyone wants to be a leader. Many very good and valuable workers simply want to be team players. But they know what they want in the way of a leader. We spell it out as ASH.

## Authenticity

*A* stands for authentic. Your outside must match your inside. Your walk must line up with your talk. You can call this authenticity or integrity or transparency. The deeper we go into the twenty-first century, the more important authenticity becomes. Cynicism among the "followers" both in the church and corporate America is at an all-time high. Sex scandals, financial improprieties, ethical illusions, and misuse of power—to name a few—have given leaders a bad name inside and outside the church.

One of the biggest enemies of authenticity is arrogance—the attitude that you have arrived. None of us knows everything. We all can still learn from others. When you stop learning, you stop becoming a leader that the best people want to follow. In order to become and then remain authentic toward those you work with, as a leader you'll need three people in your life:

- a coach to tell you what you are supposed to be doing
- a counselor with whom you can discuss your feelings
- a choreographer who can show you how what you are doing is being perceived by your stakeholders

## Self-Awareness

*S* stands for self-awareness. You need to have a clear understanding of what makes you the person you are. This is "standing naked in front of the mirror" time. What are your strengths? (We all like this part.) What are your weak areas? (We like to skip this part.) Then develop a plan that helps you relate to your teammates in light of your strengths and weaknesses.

This is a difficult, but necessary, assessment. None of us likes to have our weaknesses exposed. My (Kirbyjon) wife had one of "those" talks with me several years ago. Usually she calls me "honey" or "baby." This time she called me "Kirbyjon."

She said, "Kirbyjon, you are a workaholic." Now, I didn't take that well at all. Me? A workaholic?

There was a reason my wife's comment stuck on me. It's the same reason a coat sticks on a hook that protrudes from the wall. If there is no hook, and you throw your coat against the wall, it falls freely to the floor. But if there's a hook sticking out from the wall and your coat hits that wall, it will hang there. When someone close to you—maybe even yourself—reveals a flaw or weakness in you, and it sticks, be assured there is a hook. Find a way to address the weakness in order to be a stronger leader.

## Humility

*H* is for humility. When your authenticity and self-awareness are out of alignment, you can't walk in humility. Humility is seeing yourself as you truly are—not more, not less. It is the realization that there is a God, and you are not Him.

If you don't walk humbly before your teammates, the best ones will leave you. The worst ones will follow you. And the rest will simply play the system as a way to draw a paycheck. That's not a team, it's just a way for unmotivated people to spend their working hours.

———————

No one person has it all. Some of us are visionaries. Others are strategists. It is vital that visionaries surround themselves with those who can implement the vision. (For a detailed discussion of building your dream team, see chapter 20.)

Remember, without the best people around you, your vision will remain simply an unfulfilled dream. If you want your vision to become reality, surround yourself with the best.

# PART IV

# THE FAITH OF AN ENTREPRENEUR

# SIXTEEN

# A REASON TO BELIEVE

## How to Put Faith Behind Your Vision

The puddles on the beach left over from the night's rain were already frozen. With the wind blowing more than twenty miles per hour, the temperature felt close to zero. Yet the two brothers were out there in the wind, wearing coats and ties no less. The conditions were not perfect, but they had told their father they would be home by Christmas, so today would have to do.

They hoisted the red flag at 10 a.m., signaling they were going ahead with the plan. Ducking in and out of their tents gave them a brief respite from the bone-chilling cold. Soon other men arrived, and with their help the brothers were able to get the craft on the launching strip heading into the wind.

After setting up a box camera to capture the event, Orville shook his brother's hand, holding the grip longer than usual. One of the onlookers later commented that it was the kind of handshake that came when two friends were parting, unsure that they would ever see each other again. Orville then climbed into the harness on the bottom wing and signed with his hand that he was ready. His brother, Wilbur, told the others not to look so sad, but to clap and cheer for Orville when he started.

It was 10:35 a.m. on December 17, 1903, at Kitty Hawk, North Carolina. The Wright brothers, from Dayton, Ohio, were about to see the fulfillment of their vision. Many said it wouldn't work. Others said they would probably meet their death in this machine. And still others held that man was not meant to fly.

Oh, how wrong they all were.

Over the next few hours, Orville and Wilbur took turns flying their heavier-than-air, powered ship over the sand dunes of Kitty Hawk. The final flight lasted nearly one minute and saw Wilbur fly 852 feet. Not bad for a first day of flying.

Orville and Wilbur Wright had a great vision, a vision that led to the discovery of "wing warping," the technique that makes it possible to control an aircraft in motion. But if it had simply ended with their vision, we would all have "frequent busing" miles to try to use for our vacation trips. The Wright brothers added faith to their vision. Without faith, our dreams will never get off the ground.

## Believing Is Seeing

Believing in what we cannot see does not come naturally. As a matter of fact, everything inside of us cries out, "This is impossible!" We need help to believe. We cry out, as the man who needed a miracle from Jesus cried, "I do believe, but help me not to doubt!" (Mark 9:24).

God does help us believe. He gives us the gift of faith. And since it's a gift, we can't do anything to earn it. We receive faith freely from God, but we have to choose whether we will use and develop this gift.

Faith is not wishing that something we want will come true. Faith is a function of our connection with God. Faith is trusting God to do what He said. Faith for an entrepreneur is believing that it is God's responsibility to bring into existence the vision He gives. Faith is not doing what we want to do—it is not even doing what we believe God wants us to do. Faith is believing that God will do what He said He will do—and that He'll include us in the process.

## GET A FAITH ALIGNMENT

If your wheels are out of alignment, you have to fight the steering wheel to keep driving in a straight line. It wears you out. By the time you reach your destination (if you get there), you're exhausted from constantly trying to stay on course.

Likewise, if your faith is out of alignment, you will find yourself fighting to keep on God's path. Even if you arrive where God wants you to be, you'll be worn out from constantly checking to see if you are still in God's will. If this is you, it's time for a faith alignment.

First, understand that faith is not hoping for a good outcome. It is not a good-luck charm. Faith is not a way to manipulate God into doing what you want. And neither is it a feeling that you work up. Instead, faith is a decision to align your will with God's will, believing that what God has planned for you is the best plan for you. By aligning your will with God's desires for your future, and by walking daily in obedience to the vision He has placed in your heart, you will find the impossible becoming not only possible, but becoming a visible reality.

It is a daily decision that each of us has to make. Will we choose to trust God for all that will come our way today? Will we choose to believe that the vision He has put in our hearts will come to pass? Every day we choose either a faith walk or a fear stop. Each is the anticipation of a future event. The one we choose to follow will determine our course in life. We walk by faith, moving forward toward a destination. But fear holds us back, causing us to lie down where we are. With fear in control, all progress stops.

Here are some practical ways to strengthen your faith walk each day, beginning with what comes out of your mouth, including what you say to others and to yourself.

## Speak Words of Faith

Somehow our tongues seem to be tied directly to our hearts. Jesus, of course, knew this when He said that the words that leave our mouths originate in the heart (see Matthew 12:34). In other words, whenever we speak, we are giving others a glimpse into our heart.

Speaking your vision is incredibly important. It not only reminds you of your mission and builds up your faith, it also builds the faith of those around you. How well do you know your mission? Can you speak it forth clearly and freely?

During World War II, if a soldier encountered a stranger he suspected of being the enemy wearing an allied uniform, he would ask, "What is your mission?" If the other soldier couldn't answer immediately, he would be arrested or shot. If you were asked, at the point of death, "What is your mission for God?" how would you answer? Would you be shot for not being able to articulate your mission?

What you talk about shows what is in your heart. And what you talk about most often shows what is foremost on your heart. If you speak often of your vision and what you're doing today to bring it to pass, others will know how important this is to you and will be more willing to join you. But if you seldom mention the vision, you must ask yourself how important it is to you. If *you're* not excited about the venture, why should others join you?

The one thing that could hold you back from talking about your vision is fear—fear that you are on the wrong path, fear that you don't have the ability to make it happen, fear that others will disagree with you or ridicule your heart's desire. But if you're going to let fear drive your life, you will accomplish nothing. Sure, you may fail a few times—maybe a lot of times—on your way to success, but at least you're moving toward your goal. Don't let fear keep you from speaking your dreams. This is how you build your faith, and faith drives fear back into the pit from which it came.

## Find a Walking Partner

Those who walk for exercise like to find partners to help them keep walking when the going gets tough. If you want to build a routine of walking each morning, what will you do the first time it's raining? Or the morning after you've been up late the night before? If you have a walking partner, there's someone to hold you accountable and encourage you through the hard times.

As a faith entrepreneur, you are sure to face hard times. But you don't have to face the hard times alone. Find others who will join you on your faith walk. Life was not meant to do alone.

The apostle Paul had a mission to accomplish. He wanted to go to Jerusalem to preach the gospel of Jesus. He heard from many well-meaning people that this was a bad idea. He should stick to what was already working. But he kept walking toward the goal. When he got to Jerusalem, things went from bad to worse. He was beaten and arrested. But he kept walking in faith, encouraged by his faith-walking partners such as Dr. Luke, Aquila and Priscilla, Timothy, and others. Walking by faith is not as hard when you have partners on the journey.

## Look Around—You're Not Alone

Entrepreneurs are known as trailblazers. While this may be true in some respects, there is nothing truly new under the sun. Someone, somewhere, at some time, has been over this ground already.

Know that others have walked this path before you, even if you feel as if you are charting completely new territory. Seek out the stories of those who have gone before, stories easily found in books and magazines. Be encouraged by their successes—and even by their failures. We have included a recommended-reading list at the end of this book. Look it over to find resources that will help you as you walk out your faith.

# SEVENTEEN

# DON'T ASK WHAT
# JESUS WOULD DO

## Instead, Ask What Jesus Is Doing—
## A Walt Kallestad Chapter

**R**efining moments are defining moments, and in 1989, sitting in a hotel room in Dallas, I was at a crossroads. Our sanctuary seated nine hundred people, and we were running five services every weekend in an attempt to keep up with the growth. The pace was grinding and relentless—fifty-minute services with next to no turnaround time. "Count 'em out, ride 'em in"—that's how it felt.

We were close to completing a new Family Life Center to accommodate the growth of our youth ministry. But even as we were nearing the completion of that building, it was clear that from day one it wouldn't be large enough.

The Sunday before, one hundred cars had driven away because there was no room to park. We were landlocked—there was no more room to grow, and we were exhausted from the pace of multiple services. But relocation seemed equally fraught with difficulty. I sensed that God wanted us to relocate, but the facts were undeniable. We were already stretched financially where we were. No room in the inn and no funds for a new one.

As we walked out our commitment and calling to be a mission church, I knew that God was calling us to provide a school and many other things for our community. That meant a campus of at least one hundred acres—probably more. But even if we had more land, there still would be the planning and the site work and the roads and utilities and buildings and the staff to utilize the buildings and the systems to recruit, train, calibrate, and supervise the staff. And that's just for starters.

I was already working my heart out, how could I do more? And beyond all of that, I knew that the decision to relocate was a $100 million decision—and that was a realm of high finance that I had never ventured anywhere near. I was in the valley of decision where the options were intimidating, but I wasn't intimidated. My mind was restless, but my spirit was at rest.

In other words, I was on the verge of a miracle.

## WE LISTEN TO THE MARKET—AND WE LISTEN TO THE MASTER

I was working on my doctor of ministry degree through Fuller Seminary, and I was in Dallas taking courses. The classes were excellent, but throughout the day I had a growing sense that I had to seek the Lord through prayer and fasting. One chapter in our church's ministry was ending, and a new one was about to begin. In my uncertainty about this new chapter, I needed to know what was on God's mind, and I knew He wanted to tell me. After all, He promised in His Word: "You are permitted to understand the secret about the Kingdom of God" (Mark 4:11).

As soon as class was over, I skipped dinner and retreated to my room. It was a cold, clear night—winter in Dallas, and the sun had already gone down. From my hotel-room window, it seemed as if all of Dallas was on display before me.

Most big cities are beautiful at night, but few cities compare with the beauty of Dallas. It's like Christmas and the Fourth of July combined, between the greens and the crisscrossing of the downtown lights, the upward-straining summits of the high rises and Reunion Tower, which looks like a firework frozen in space. I love looking at city skylines by night because they are at once teeming with energy and yet somehow peaceful and inviting—like the power of God.

With this beautiful panorama spread out before me, I dropped to my knees and began to pray. And as I prayed, I began to write. Rapid fire. Non-stop. Four hours went by before I looked up. God was revealing His vision for the next chapter in our ministry—and today we're doing what He revealed to me in 1989.

And here's the beauty of all this: When you draw near to God and do what He tells you to do, it not only ushers you into His blessing, *it gives you courage.* You see, on more than one occasion it has seemed like things were falling apart, and I didn't know where our next dime was coming from. But I knew in my heart that I had been obedient, and that God surely would come through. And you know what? He always has, and He always will. And what He does for me, *He will surely do for you.*

## What Is Jesus Doing?

According to Peter Drucker, there is only one definition of an entrepreneur: "An entrepreneur is someone who gets something new done."[1] So how do we as spiritual entrepreneurs do new things? We can either *decide* what we want or *discern* what God wants.

When we *decide,* we evaluate the options before us and choose which one to pursue. We might study demographics and psychographics. We might take a survey or a vote. Hey, we might even cut a deck of cards. And if we're spiritual, at the end we may even ask God to bless what we've decided to do without first praying about it. This is a prescription for powerlessness.

The entrepreneur of faith wants instead to *discern,* to move forward in the power of God, to follow Him in doing something new. One of the most remarkable passages in the Bible is Isaiah 43:19, where the Lord says: "See, I am doing a new thing! Now it springs up; do you not perceive it? I am making a way in the desert and streams in the wasteland" (NIV). There are three vitally important principles here.

First, God is already at work all around us. He has a plan, He is actively at work fulfilling that plan, and that plan involves *new things.*

Second, it's our job to perceive the new things that God is doing. The Hebrew word translated *perceive* means "to know" (properly to ascertain by *seeing*). You receive tremendous power for life and ministry when you trade deciding for discerning. When we *discern* what God is doing and join it, we enter into a zone of blessing. We don't have to ask Him to bless what we're doing; instead, we enter into what He's *already* blessing. That's why it's so important to ask and answer the question, "What is Jesus doing?" And more than ask it—start doing what He's doing.

Third, the new things that God is doing are *wonderful.* There are more Christians alive today than in all the previous eras of church history combined. Christians make up a larger percentage of the world's population than they ever have. Compared to 1900, today we:

- have nine times more churches;
- distribute almost eleven times more Bibles;
- have five times more vocational Christian workers;
- have nearly seven times more missionaries;
- have one hundred and sixty times more Christian books;
- spend thirty-six times more hours in evangelizing;

- have cut the proportion of unevangelized people in the world in half;[2]
- are broadcasting the Great Good News of Jesus Christ via television, radio, the Internet, and the media to every city, county, country, and continent; and
- are seeing our young people poised to do a dramatically better job in reaching the world than we have done.

This is the Lord's doing, and it is marvelous in our eyes! So how do we discern what Jesus is doing?

## How to Find Out What God's Doing

Here is the cross-your-heart-and-hope-to-die, top-secret, highly confidential method for finding out what God is doing in your world. Brace yourself.

*You ask God, and He tells you.* God makes this incredible promise to us: "Call to me and I will answer you and tell you great and unsearchable things you do not know" (Jeremiah 33:3, NIV).

Let's take God at His Word. Let's assume He means what He says. He tells us to call to Him. He promises that if we do, He will tell us "great and unsearchable things," things we'd never come up with on our own. But to hear this amazing thing from God, after we ask we have to listen. More to the point, we have to take time to listen. I know that, like me, you're probably going mach three with your hair on fire. You've got way more to do than you have time for—and you like it that way. A lot.

It's time to slow down, occasionally to stop completely, so you can listen to God. Here's how I draw near so I can listen for His voice:

- I remove all distractions. That's pretty obvious isn't it? You're not going to hear the still, small voice while you're talking on your cell phone while listening to the radio while eating a donut while driving to the office.

- Then I become still and quiet. With all due (or undue) respect to Joan Rivers, enter listening. Keeping a prayer journal can help with this. God is going to speak to you, and you don't want to forget what He says.

- I take the necessary time. Since you're reading this book, I'm guessing you're a leader. If not at work, then in the church. If not on staff, then in a volunteer position. If not on a grand scale, then on a committee or some quiet ministry. You love God and you love doing His work. You're committed and conscientious and probably have taken on too much. We are so busy and so involved and running so fast that we easily fall into the trap of prayerless activity. And before we know it, we've forgotten how to hear God's voice or even what to do in His presence. But here's the beauty of prayer: The more you pray, the more you want to pray. Pray sixty seconds—soon you'll be praying for five minutes. Pray five minutes, and soon you'll be praying half an hour. That's the beauty of being in God's presence, and the beauty of drawing near to Him.

- I make sure to spend *consistent* time with God. The first thing I do every morning is get down on my knees and pray. Every afternoon I take time out for prayer. The busier my schedule, the more time I allow for prayer. For real.

God both speaks to us and shows us. He will tell you what He wants you to do—and show you, often by the success or failure of a venture. Some people ask: Is God calling us to be faithful or successful? The answer is simple: He's calling us to be both.

The Spirit of God lives in you, the power of God flows through you, the promises of God are prepared for you, the voice of God guides you, the angels of God protect you, and the armor of God equips you. Do you really think God does all that so we can live mediocre lives doing mediocre things with mediocre results? Of course you don't. So be faithful to unleash the success that God has ordained for you before the foundation of the world.

# EIGHTEEN

# YOU CALL THAT SUCCESS?

## How God Measures Results

Most of us won't admit it, but we love comparison, especially if our own accomplishments rise to the top of the heap. We love coming out on top. We want others to consider us winners, successful in whatever we do. After all, what creative, passionate person (in other words, what entrepreneur) longs to be average? We want to excel, to make a difference, to succeed. And, what is success?

That question is hard enough to answer in the business world. Is success measured monthly, quarterly, or annually? How do you measure the revenues generated by new stores against income produced by existing stores? Is it gross or net? And should success be measured only by comparing a store with its own results in the same quarter last year?

But just what is success in the Kingdom of God? In the scope of eternity and in the realm of God's Kingdom, how is success measured? Is it by the number of people who attend each week or by the amount of the offerings? Perhaps it's determined by the size and scope of a ministry. Wouldn't a ministry that has a nationwide reach be more successful than one that "only" serves a single city or a part of a city? And of course, an international ministry would trump a national program. But then how do we measure an outreach that extends only to one neighborhood? Even if great good is being done, can we really consider such a modest ministry to be a "success"?

## JESUS WEIGHS IN

Jesus knew these things would be on our minds. After all, two of His closest followers came to Him asking for the honor of sitting at Jesus's side once they all arrived in heaven. And if those guys, who spent three years with Jesus, were compelled to request a place of honor in heaven, it's guaranteed that the matter of success, and comparisons, will at least cross our minds.

So, to help us gain a godly perspective on these matters, Jesus addressed the subject of success with two stories. It's good for us to hear these stories again.

### The Two Sons

Jesus told of two sons who were called into their father's presence. The father looked at the first son and said, "I have something for you to do."

This son told his father that he had plenty of things to do that were more important. His time was valuable, after all. Then he grunted, shrugged his shoulders, and sauntered off. What an attitude!

Then the second son walked in, and the father said, "I have something for you to do."

"Cool, Dad," the son responded. "I'll get right on it." He hugged his father warmly and walked away with a big smile on his face. But he never got around to doing what his father had asked.

I suppose it's easy to see which of these sons was the successful one in his father's eyes. That is, until you read that the first son ended up doing exactly what the father had asked of him, but the second son did not obey. Which is the successful son? The first, of course. Here, success is measured by obedience. The first son obeyed his father, even if his attitude was questionable (see Matthew 21:28-32).

## Investing for the Master

Jesus's second story had to do with a businessman getting ready to leave on an extended trip. He called three of his servants into his office. There, he gave each of the men an amount of money. The first got five thousand dollars, the second got two thousand, and the third got one thousand. Each servant was instructed to invest the money for the boss, since it belonged to him.

When the businessman returned from his journey, he called the servants to his office. "How did you make out with my money?" he asked each one.

The first servant reported on his financial dealings. "I took a big gamble," he admitted. "I invested all five thousand dollars. I could have lost it all, but I made another five thousand to match what I started out with. Here you are—ten thousand dollars."

"Great job!" said the businessman. "I now have more money for you to invest for me."

The second servant stepped forward.

"My story is the same as my friend's," he began. "I invested all of the two thousand dollars that you gave me. I know it was a risk, but I made an additional two thousand. Here is your four thousand dollars."

Again, the businessman rewarded the servant with more money to be invested.

Now it was time for the third servant to report on his activities. He had already heard the other two guys explain how they had doubled their boss's money. The third servant gulped and rose slowly to his feet.

"Well?" asked the businessman.

The servant held out a stack of bills totaling one thousand dollars.

"That's the money I gave you before I left on my trip!" the businessman shouted. "Why didn't you use it to make me more money?"

"Well, you see," stammered the servant, "I thought about investing it, but I was afraid. I mean, what would happen if the market went south and I lost your money? So rather than take such a big risk, I buried it in a safe place. See, here is the money you left with me. It's all here."

The businessman knew that he had lost money—perhaps as much as one thousand additional dollars, because the third servant failed to invest the money. The third servant was fired immediately, and with no severance pay (see Matthew 25:14-30).

Of course we see that the two servants who invested their master's money were the successful ones. Why? Because they exercised faith.


## HOW GOD MEASURES SUCCESS

Obedience and faith. These are the two ways God measures our success. And they're the only ways that spiritual entrepreneurs can measure their own success. Have you been obedient to what God has called you to do? And did you carry out this assignment in faith, leaving the results to God? If so, you can count your venture a success. Don't worry about numbers, budgets, news coverage, speaking invitations, or awards. They don't count when God is measuring the success of a faith venture.

You might be leading a small venture that God considers one of this year's greatest successes. But you won't know about it. You will never see your ultimate success in this life. Read again the stories of the heroes of faith recorded in the eleventh chapter of Hebrews. These men and women were obedient and faithful. But many of them died cruel, agonizing deaths as they took stands for God. They didn't see the heights of their successes until they left this life. And the same is true for knowing the true impact of your ministry. Like the heroes of Hebrews 11, you, too, are part of a major success story.

Our role is to believe and obey. If we do these two things, we can count ourselves successful. That is the only comparison that counts.

# PART V

## THE WORK
## OF A SPIRITUAL
## ENTREPRENEUR

# NINETEEN

# ENTREPRENEURIAL FAITH
# WITHOUT WORK IS DEAD

## God Called You, So Don't Give Up

A
s we have said before, spiritual entrepreneurs are persons who see what God wants them to see, believe in what they see, and do it. Up to this point we've talked about seeing what God wants us to see—*vision*—and then believing in what we see—*faith*. Now it's time to get to work, to act in faith on what God has shown us.

James, the brother of Jesus, made this succinct statement in his letter to the early church: Faith without works is dead (see James 2:17). Someone who declares his vision and believes that the vision can and should come to be, yet never puts plans into motion to make the vision a reality, has dead faith. Alive faith acts with courage to implement your vision.

## God's Vision Is Inconvenient

Mary was looking forward to becoming Joseph's wife. He was a kind man, and his carpentry work would provide a steady income. It would be enough for Mary to make a good home for their children. Her future was bright, especially when compared to girls who could not, for one reason or another, marry. And she was certainly in a better position than the slaves who served her family. Yes, she was looking forward to being Joseph's wife.

Then God came into her life and really messed things up. She was pregnant but not married. And she was the only one who knew the truth of how she had become pregnant. What would Joseph think? If he annulled their betrothal, how would Mary survive? She would certainly be treated as an outcast, even by her family. Things had been going so smoothly until God had come in.

Have you ever felt like Mary? Things are flowing just fine in your career, your family, your church or organization. Then God puts a vision in your heart and you believe this is what God would have you pursue. The reaction of those around you can be much like it must have been when Mary announced she was going to have God's baby. "You've got to be kidding!"

Acting with entrepreneurial faith is not a solitary endeavor. It's not meant to be walked out by yourself, but that's how you may feel—alone—when you're starting to put your vision into action. Your boss may think you're nuts for leaving a secure, well-paying job to become a preacher.[1] Your congregation may vote with their feet when you redirect certain ministries in order to start reaching the unchurched. I (Walt) am the expert in "growing" a congregation from two hundred to one hundred attendees.[2] And your family. What if putting your vision into action means pulling up roots and moving? Or that you will have to work two jobs for a season? How do you convince those around you that you really have heard from God, and you are simply obeying what He told you to do? That was Mary's predicament. And it is repeated today in the lives of untold numbers of spiritual entrepreneurs.

The fact is, you can't prove to anyone else what God has shown you. They have to hear from God themselves. In the meantime, your passion and persistence will help them "buy into" your vision. You may feel as if you're walking the road alone. You may feel that God's calling is messing everything up. But it's up to you, by faith, to decide you will obey God and do what He has called you to do. Obedience puts faith into action.

## Grow Like a Tree

The wind howls, knocking over signs and blowing shingles off the roof. Your lawn furniture ends up in your neighbor's yard. Yet that oak tree in your backyard stays put. The branches swing and sway, but in the morning it's still standing. How do trees survive what other plants and man-made objects cannot? The answer is simple: roots.

The root system of a tree, as well as most other plants, grows underground long before you see much evidence of growth above ground. It's this strong and extensive root system that allows the tree to endure harsh winds. Roots go deep in search of water, so in times of drought the tree can survive. Any plant, be it a pansy or a massive sugar maple, that does not have a good root system will not survive the hard times.

Your first actions in your entrepreneurial venture may be unseen by most. Before you go public with your vision—taking it above ground where it will be examined—you must spend time in research and planning. (For a detailed discussion of feasibility studies, see appendix A.) That's how you put down the necessary roots. Be patient. Don't try to create a full-sized, mature ministry overnight.

There are many good books available that give detailed instructions on how to prepare a business plan. Two that we recommend are *Business Plans for Dummies* by Paul Tiffany and Steven Peterson, and *The Successful Business Plan: Secrets and Strategies* by Rhonda Abrams. Get several of these from your local library or bookstore or purchase a software package that walks you through the process of preparing a business plan. It's important to try out your vision on paper before you begin building above ground. (To look at a sample business plan used by Community Church of Joy, see appendix B.)

## THERE IS NO PERFECT PLAN

We want to offer two words of advice here about strategic plans. First, being an entrepreneur means you really like to *do* things. You are internally wired to shoot now and aim later. Sitting down to read about, then write out, a business plan is as exciting to you as trying to watch a tree grow. Since we feel so strongly about planning before you leap, here is some good advice: Find someone who loves making business plans and let that person do it.

This means unveiling—if even just a little—your vision. You will be letting someone else take a close look at your baby. This is a good thing. We are not meant to carry out a vision alone. Entrepreneurial faith is a communal venture, just like the body of Christ is a community of faith. In the following chapter we will talk about the importance of building your dream team. For now, it's enough to let one person in on your dreams to help you assess the viability of your vision.

The other warning we want to issue regarding business or strategic plans may be obvious, but we need to say it anyway. You can make the best, most detailed spreadsheet showing the pluses and minuses of your vision and *still* something will go wrong. There are always going to be unforeseen circumstances that will require you to make adjustments. Don't think of your plan as chiseled in stone, but rather as wet cement that still needs shaping and smoothing.

## DON'T CLING TO THE SEED

If you plant a hickory seed in the ground, you expect a hickory tree to grow in that spot. But before growth can begin, the seed must die. The outer skin of the seed needs to degrade, allowing the "hot" center to come to life and begin the tree's growth cycle.

In the same way, you most likely will find a time when your dream seems like it has died. Perhaps it never gets off the ground, or perhaps it is growing but you can't yet see evidence of that. In any case, your vision needs to experience death before it truly comes to life. In God's world, death leads to rebirth.

Jesus, of course, is our example in this paradox of life. He compared Himself to a seed that had to die before it could live (see John 12:24). Jesus died, then rose to life, opening the door for all of us to follow Him into Real Life. With Jesus as our model, we need to embrace the paradox—let our dreams die, and then see God bring them to life. Don't hold tightly to your dream as if it "belongs" to you. Be willing to let it die if that's what God brings about.

## IT DON'T COME EASY

Ringo Starr was absolutely right when he sang, "It don't come easy."[3] Very little in this life that is worth having does come easy. Bringing your dream into reality will take a lot of hard work by you and those you recruit to your "dream team."

If you go into this venture without counting the cost, you may quickly give up. If you fail to prepare for a hard climb, the mountain looming before you may seem insurmountable. You might turn back, letting your vision go unfulfilled. The saying "Work smarter, not harder" is not entirely correct. A lot of the time you'll need to roll up your sleeves and work hard. Really hard. Harder than you bargained for when God gave you the vision.

On the other hand, if you begin the task prepared to work long and hard, it will not seem quite as long or feel as hard as you thought.

## Develop Bulldog Perseverance

You have no doubt heard the sarcastic saying, "Just what part of 'no' do you not understand?" The most accurate answer an entrepreneur can give is, "All of it."

If you give up quickly when you run up against a no, you will not last long as a builder of new things. A high percentage of new businesses fail within the first five years. What is the key to the five percent that hang in there? Persistence. Persistence is a vital quality for an entrepreneur.

Think about a bulldog. God made the bulldog in such a way that he has incredible persistence in a fight. Most dogs can't keep a grip with their jaws for long. They have to let go in order to breathe. But the bulldog's nose slants backward so that the dog can continue to breathe as it keeps its jaws locked on its adversary.

Napoleon Hill, author of *Think and Grow Rich,* said, "The majority of people meet with failure because of their lack of persistence in creating new plans to take the place of those which fail."[4] The spiritual entrepreneur must never give up. When all else is done, stand.

# TWENTY

# CREATING YOUR DREAM TEAM

## Don't Attempt the Entrepreneurial Life Alone

t's another Sunday morning, and you're looking out over your congregation. You've been thinking about who you can recruit to be a part of your
entrepreneurial team. Who are the best people to help you carry out your
dream? Even if no one comes to mind, rest assured that your teammates are
out there. Here's how you can spot them: Everyone in your church is to be
on your entrepreneurial team.

That's right. *Everyone.*

### DEVELOPING ENTREPRENEURS

One of the most important, and most enjoyable, jobs you have as an entrepreneurial leader is creating an entrepreneurial atmosphere. This is more vital
than finding new opportunities for growth or dreaming of possibilities or
pursuing new visions. If you fail to create an entrepreneurial atmosphere that
encourages everyone to carry out entrepreneurial tasks, then you are failing as

a leader. Everyone in your organization or church must be primed to constantly look for new growth areas and also be willing to let go of nonproductive programs and projects.

An entrepreneurial church, organization, or committee does not limit entrepreneurial action only to the few people the leader invites into his or her inner circle. As a matter of fact, if you're to be a true entrepreneur or faith, you have to forget the idea of an "inner circle" entirely. Top-down management is not the way an entrepreneurial organization operates. Entrepreneurship is a team sport where the offensive lineman has just as important a role in victory as does the quarterback or the wide receiver.

## There's One Now!

How can you spot a church where the pastor has created an entrepreneurial atmosphere? The staff arrives to work most every day filled with anticipation at what exciting things will take place. There's energy and excitement from the senior pastor to the sexton. The congregation knows they not only have the right but also the obligation to find new ways to carry out the church's mission. And everyone in the church knows that people are much more important than programs.

This kind of church or organization does not just happen. It takes a leader to guide both the staff and the volunteers to this new way of thinking, believing, and acting. At first, your staff and congregation may react negatively. You are introducing the dreaded *c* word—change. You will need to constantly remind them, as well as yourself, what Albert Einstein said: "You cannot solve a problem using the same mindset that created it."

## The Leader's Daily Practice

In order to create your dream team—one that is energetic and purposeful in seeking new ideas—you first need to daily exhibit the habits of highly productive entrepreneurs. Your staff and church members will take their lead from you. So you must act at all times as you want your team to act.

## Take Time to Dream

Is a large part of your time set aside to pursue new models of ministry? Are you relentless in your pursuit of new dreams? Do you try, then sometimes fail, and then get up to try again? Do you allow yourself to dream, even if the dream seems impossible? If you are not doing these things in a highly visible way, how can you expect your team to do them?

Dreaming and vision building will never happen if you fail to purposefully set aside enough time. The hours in your days can easily be consumed by the everyday events that call for your time and attention. If you're to see clearly the vision God wants to show you, you must learn to periodically shut your eyes to what's going on around you.

The 3M Company allows every employee to use 15 percent of his or her time dreaming of new ways to do a task or to come up with new products and services that will benefit their customers. Are you giving yourself at least one day each week to dream? I (Walt) set aside Friday as my "dream day." It is often the most important, and most productive, day of my week.

If you are practicing regular dreaming, your team will follow suit. It will become second nature to them to set aside time to entertain new visions. They will then follow your lead in relentlessly pursuing those visions.

## Promote Risk Taking

You must allow all your teammates to take wise risks without fear of reprisal. Does everyone on your team know that failure is acceptable as long as they, as John Maxwell puts it, "fail forward"?[1] Some staff members will need more encouragement than others to feel the freedom to take risks. Others may be so eager for change that they become reckless. They might need some counseling on the aspect of taking *wise* risks. But you are the one who will create the climate that encourages everyone to try.

## Be a Road Builder

The third behavior you must model is that of a road builder. Too many leaders become firefighters, since there are so many fires to be put out every day. After answering fire alarms all day, the leader goes home exhausted. He or she was running all day long, throwing water on one hot spot just to watch another erupt later in the day.

Instead of fighting fires, you need to be about the business of building roads. Entrepreneurs find new paths to get from here to there—that's their job. In order to do this job, you need to develop a team of road builders, all of whom are equipped to find new paths to better accomplish the mission.

## Plug into the Power of Passion

If you still question the importance of operating from within a team, think about the model Jesus established. Jesus, the Ultimate Entrepreneur, knew that life is not a solo flight. He understood that we need others to partner with us in carrying out our vision and following God's calling. Jesus handselected a group of ordinary men. None of the twelve disciples was a public speaker or a trained theologian. None would be identified as an influential figure in first-century Palestine. Jesus didn't select them based on their expertise or their social or political connections or their wealth.

Instead, Jesus selected a ragged group of blue-collar workers, political zealots, and social outcasts, mentored them into a team, then empowered them to share God's good news. And it changed the world. On the outside, these guys didn't have much going for them. But what Jesus saw in them was passion, perhaps the most vital characteristic for a member of a successful entrepreneurial team. Jesus trained them in His ways, but He didn't quench their individuality. And think about the result!

After Jesus accomplished His mission and was once again seated at the right hand of God, these "trainees" continued to spread the message, taking it to all corners of the earth. That's success, by any measure.

## DREAM TEAMS HELP YOU FOCUS

As we talk about the necessity of working from within a team and the importance of building roads versus fighting fires, we must also acknowledge the reality of fires. Most of them need to be extinguished so they won't consume the good that you're trying to accomplish. But a few of them can actually be beneficial.

Farmers burn their fields in order to turn spent crops into valuable nitrogen that can be plowed back into the soil. Forest fires that are started by natural causes (as opposed to someone's tossing a lit match into the brush) can clear out dead trees and undergrowth that keep new trees and plants from reaching their full potential. Could some of the fires you spend so much time dousing actually be better for your organization in the long run if you simply let them burn themselves out?

Other fires pose a real threat. They rage and grow, consuming more and more fuel. They need to be extinguished, but that doesn't mean that *you* have to be the firefighter. As the lead entrepreneur, you must assess your strengths and weaknesses and then focus on using your strengths while compensating for your weaknesses. Utilize your team members in areas that will free you up to focus on core strengths and activities, such as road building.

Who on your team is best suited to fight fires? And how can a person in that role help the team operate more effectively? As you think through who can serve as fire captain, realize that fighting fires is an entrepreneurial task. Red Adair has made a small fortune from putting out oil-well fires. He is the recognized specialist in that area. With Adair in charge of capping burning oil wells, the oil companies can concentrate on new ways to find, extract, and refine petroleum. And through the years, Adair has found new and better ways to fight these dangerous fires. That's entrepreneurship. His methods are now taught to firefighters the world over. In this model, everyone wins.

In your own setting, recruit a team member who is gifted as a trouble-shooter. He or she can become the fire captain, responding to 911 calls as new flames flare up. Finding that person and giving him or her the freedom to operate gets you off the fire truck so you can spend your best thinking and energy building roads.

# TWENTY-ONE

# THE DISCIPLINE OF FOCUS

## Limitations That Maximize Your Creativity

W e are firm believers in the truth that without discipline you'll never multiply your creativity. You might disagree, reasoning that it's not realistic, or even appropriate, to mix discipline with creativity. After all, isn't creativity the freedom to dream big without the defeating constraints and limitations of outside forces? Doesn't discipline just shove you back into a rut, defeating the creative spirit?

We're familiar with this argument. But is it really true?

Imagine that you want to put in a sidewalk leading from your driveway to your front door. You mix the concrete and pour it on the ground, right? Well, that could create some interesting piles of concrete, and perhaps even a unique design. But it most certainly won't give you the sidewalk you envisioned.

First, you must lay down boards to use as concrete forms to hold the wet cement along the path where you want the sidewalk. Then you pour the cement between the forms—and only between the forms. Anything that spills outside the boards has to be cleaned up.

You might argue that we're using the wrong analogy: "A sidewalk is merely functional, a mundane creation designed to serve a practical purpose. We're not launching new sidewalks here, we're dreaming big dreams and seeing amazing visions. Our work is way too big and too important to tether to the ground with discipline. How can we have unfettered creativity if you insist on imposing strict boundaries?"

Well, let's stick with the sidewalk illustration for a moment longer. You've rethought the whole thing, and instead of running the sidewalk straight from the driveway to the front door, you now want visitors to be able to see your prized flower garden as they approach the house. So you need the walk to wind through the flower beds. And instead of a drab, gray-colored walk, you decide to use one of the new colored concretes—perhaps even to create a pattern of shades and colors.

It might be "just a sidewalk," but you have almost unlimited options. But no matter how far afield your thinking might go as you decide the particulars, your creativity is still bounded by a few givens. You need to create a walkway from the driveway to the front door, so the beginning point and ending point are set. And you need a paving material that will stand up for years. Concrete, asphalt, flagstone, or bricks would seem to be the options. Expense is a consideration, of course, and so are beauty and durability. Given the available finances, concrete is the choice you land on.

Once you've settled on the paving material, the route your sidewalk will take from driveway to front door, and the color you'll use, you'll have to install the concrete forms to hold the wet cement within the boundaries of the path you choose for the walk. You have invested a tremendous amount of creativity in this process—even though it's a "routine" project.

## Forms for Your Dreams

In the same way, entrepreneurs who try to pursue every dream that pops into their heads will end up like cement poured out on the ground. Gravity will pull the wet cement downhill, into low spots and along drainage areas. You'll have a design of sorts, but it will be a rough design that may or may not add beauty and value. The one thing that is certain is that a sidewalk poured without using forms will provide little help to people who need a solid surface to walk on.

You need boundaries, even if you're an entrepreneur of the highest order. You might chafe at the idea, but in the end you'll find that boundaries put you a step ahead of the game. As a leader, you must not only set up boundaries for your own dreams and visions but also for your entire team. Those you work with will not always greet such restrictions with high-fives and expressions of gratitude. But you're the leader, so lead. Go ahead and impose wise and needed limits. Putting restrictions on a vision is uncomfortable but necessary if you hope to turn your vision into reality.

Focus is your responsibility. An entrepreneurial team will head off in all directions, each member chasing his or her specialized version of the big vision. As the leader, you need to set a focus for your team. What is it that *you* consider your primary mission? As believers, we have each received a commission to go forth and make disciples of all people. But each person, and each church, has different means to accomplish this calling. Since you're the leader, you must sort through the good things so your team can concentrate on the *best* thing—the vision that God has given you.

## Our Focal Point

We can get so caught up in bringing a vision to life through a new or improved service that we get our eyes off the end result. We get so excited about turning the dream into reality that we're consumed by the process. We zero in on the means and temporarily forget the destination. Sales reps for a line of power tools are reminded that customers don't go to a hardware store because they want a really snazzy new power drill. The customer goes to the store because he needs something that will put holes in a wall so he can install some shelves. The power drill simply supplies the means to meet the customer's need. He needs holes in a wall, drilled in a variety of sizes.

We need to focus on the holes, not the drill.

What is it that our customers—the unchurched people in our communities—really need? Do they need Sunday school or Vacation Bible School? Do they need welcoming committees or visitor follow-ups?

Rick Warren, pastor of Saddleback Church outside Los Angeles, puts it in very simple terms: "People don't need friendly churches. People need friends."[1]

What do the people in your community need? Do they need friends? Then focus your entrepreneurial efforts on finding ways to connect the unchurched in your community with people they can consider their friends. Do they need jobs? Investigate methods to create jobs, such as Windsor Village United Methodist Church did in the development of the Power Center.

Just out of college, I (Walt) was a youth worker for a church in Burnsville, Minnesota. At the time, this was one of the most desirable suburbs of Minneapolis to live in. But the school system had great needs. There was a higher-than-average incidence of teen pregnancies and suicides among the students. Drug usage was rampant. Kids were having sex in the stairwells. The need to reach these students was obvious.

I approached the school district with an idea. I suggested they hire me as a staff member, with an office on the high-school campus (and another on the junior-high campus) to reach out with a faith-based message. I organized a team to work with the students, sharing the gospel with them. I also organized weekend retreats with the students. We put on a musical every weekend called "A Natural High." Churches throughout the community came together with a common mission—to help save the students. At the height of this outreach we had at least a thousand junior-high and a thousand senior-high students involved in the program.

As a result of this work, the school district realized a great reduction in pregnancies, suicides, and drug use among students. A much safer climate was established in the school. And, most of all, many lives were won for the Kingdom.

## DON'T LET SUCCESS KILL YOUR PASSION

As you minister to others with your creativity multiplied by discipline and focus, you will find that the odds for success increase greatly. And by success, we mean effective, God-directed ministry that touches lives to meet real needs. Success, in God's economy, is a Christian faithfully living out God's calling in his or her life.

We all seek this type of success, especially after we commit to the life of entrepreneurial faith. But there is a danger hidden here as well. The danger is that after creating and implementing a new initiative that gets your church or organization into the community where it is now meeting needs, you will choose stability. You will sit back and relax with the good feeling that your vision is now reality. Your dream to help hurting people is now a significant program that is ministering grace and practical help to those in your community. You are right to appreciate and celebrate God's work through you and your team, but the danger is that you'll stay there—resting in the relative quiet of having the new initiative running under its own power.

You can stay there for a moment. There's nothing wrong with savoring the joy of seeing God work. But don't wait too long before you reenter the world of entrepreneurial faith. On earth, we will never get to the end of the Kingdom of God, so there is no time that we can say, "There. It's finally done! Now I can relax." Human needs don't take a holiday, so we can't rest from the life of entrepreneurial faith.

Bob Vaage is pastor of First Lutheran Church in Milford, Iowa. In this town of fewer than two thousand people, Bob's church is alive with entrepreneurial faith. The church grew so fast that many of the more than fourteen hundred baptized members had no place to park their cars, and no place to sit once they got inside the sanctuary. Bob and his leaders could have played it safe and bought a few more acres nearby. Instead, they bought sixty acres on a main highway. Their dream is to serve all the generations of their community, from preschoolers to the elderly, with recreation, learning, and Christ-centered ministry. A Christian-based retirement company already has bought five acres from the church and built an assisted-living center, which helped the church recover its investment in the land.

Although Vaage's congregation is just now getting ready to break ground for the first church building on their new campus, they have been using the property for worship services for two years. They are continuing a tradition the church began more than fifty years ago—an outdoor drive-in service. The church started this service at a local drive-in theater. Today, on a hillside outside Milford, not far from Lake Okoboji, hundreds of vacationers, farmers, and townsfolk drive up every summer Sunday in their swimsuits and shorts, and roll down their windows to sing along with the morning worship. As Pastor Bob preaches from atop a wooden platform, the worshipers express their gratitude by honking their horns. First Lutheran's new campus will serve summer worship in Milford for years to come. That's entrepreneurial faith.

## ENTREPRENEURIAL FOCUS

Within the approach of entrepreneurial faith, success will never be a reason to feel that the job is done. The job is *never* done, because human needs are ever-present. In fact, human needs are increasing. We're not gaining ground on solving the problem of human suffering; in fact, we're losing ground, sadly, every day.

So view your successes as added motivation to keep at it, to rethink approaches, to renew your passion and creativity in launching new initiatives. And if a program that has been in place for some time is still growing, let it keep growing. Never assume that it has already served its purpose, if it continues to grow.

Entrepreneurs don't look to retire. They look for additional opportunities for advancement. Entrepreneurial faith is not a destination—it's an ongoing journey. And as you continue on this journey, maximize your effectiveness by maintaining your focus. Here are two ways to keep your head in the game.

First, don't allow the intense effort of creating and launching new initiatives to cause you to forget the *reason* you're creating them. You must do things that will keep you connected with the needs that sparked the idea in the beginning. If you're working on a plan to match elementary school students with senior citizens as tutors and mentors, set aside time every few weeks to take some kids to the senior center for lunch. Seeing the spontaneous relationships develop between the kids and their soon-to-be mentors will fuel your passion and keep you focused as you move forward with the creation of the new program. Remember the needs as you immerse yourself in the process of creating services that will meet those needs.

And second, maintain the same focus after your bold initiatives become established, ongoing ministries. Don't sit back in ease. Don't lose your focus after you achieve success. The program will need some fine-tuning, and its success will most likely give rise to spin-off ministries that will need your leadership.

Remember, since human needs are always with us, the need for entrepreneurial faith is always there. Multiply your creativity through discipline, maintain your focus, and never allow success to dampen your entrepreneurial spirit.

# TWENTY-TWO

# THE ENTREPRENEUR'S
# ONE ESSENTIAL ACTIVITY

## Prayer: Don't Pursue a Vision Without It

We've covered a lot of ground so far, talking about the importance of receiving a vision or dream from God. We've explored how vital it is to believe what God reveals to you, and how you need to walk in faith until you fulfill the vision.

As you work to turn dreams into reality, you need certain tools in your toolbox. We've discussed leading by example and empowering the entire community (congregation, staff, and volunteers) to think and act entrepreneurially. We've looked at discipline, parameters, and focus—keeping the goal and the reason for the ministry always in front of you. You also need perseverance. A viable business plan. Willingness to work hard. A focused team of like-minded entrepreneurial souls. The list keeps growing.

But the list is not yet complete. As we near the end of this book, we land on the one essential practice that a spiritual entrepreneur absolutely cannot succeed without. This action of the entrepreneur is not optional. It's not just a quaint suggestion or something worth considering if it happens to come to mind. No, this one is foundational to everything else. Without it, you need not even open the toolbox.

The all-important tool is prayer.

We're not going to delve into the power or mystery of prayer. We trust you already have direct experience with asking God for things, sharing your heart with Him, and seeing Him work in response to your petitions. We assume that prayer has a place in your daily life.

But if you don't give prayer a high priority, please consider this: God is talking to you all the time. He loves you so much that He can't stop thinking about you. He longs for intimacy with you. He loves to listen to what is on your mind and heart. Spending time with God should not be something simply to be checked off your to-do list. Once we come to experience the awesome presence of God when we pray, we will want to quickly check off *everything else* on our agendas in order to give our Father the undivided attention He deserves.

## It's Not Your Responsibility

Praying over your visions and dreams helps you acknowledge that the outcome is God's responsibility. Committing everything to God through prayer helps you do your best work and then trust God for the impact and results. The risks and rewards of your dream are no longer in your hands. God has them now. He understands risks. He knows about rewards. He can handle yours.

Prayer transfers your visions to God. He then assumes the management of that vision. Any new venture brings its own truckload of uncertainty. An entrepreneur must face this tension when taking on a new venture. But there are no uncertainties in God. None. He can handle any idea—no matter how "out there" it seems—with complete certainty.

Your role is to hand your visions and dreams over to God for Him to handle in His way. And as you do that, why not give Him your worries as well? Wouldn't it feel great if the burden of those doubts and problems you've been carrying on your shoulders were taken away? Just think how much faster you could run!

## God Will Transform Your Dreams

If you transfer your vision to God through prayer, you are giving Him permission to transform your vision. Yes, you have a great idea for a new ministry that promises to have a tremendous impact on your community. Yet God knows the end from the beginning. He knows what is going to happen tomorrow and the day after that, and exactly how all the unforeseen developments will affect your vision. Through prayer, allow God to transform your vision in the way He knows will work best to bring about His desired results.

When you pray about your vision, you are giving God permission to do as He knows best with your plans. His ways are far above yours. Be prepared—God does not often feel the need to explain what He is doing or why He is doing it. Just remember: He is God, and you are not. Trust Him to be the loving God that He is.

## Making Prayer Practical

Here are ten practices that will help you pray regularly, and in faith, over your vision.

- *Set aside five minutes every day to pray.* It isn't necessary to pray out loud. Simply focus on God and on your dreams. This opens your mind to receive fresh insights from God.
- *Tell God in your own words about your dream.* Talk to Him like you talk to a friend. Be as specific or as general, as elaborate or as simple as you feel is needed. God understands it all.

- *Pray regularly throughout the day, as you go about the duties and activities of life.* Pray in the car or on the bus or at your desk. Imagine that God is working beside you. Anywhere you may be, you can enjoy short conversations with God—thirty-second prayers with your eyes closed to block out any distractions. The more often you do this, the more you will sense God's involvement in your life and dreams.

- *Do not always ask for something, but spend time thanking God for everything*—and we do mean *everything.* Thank him for small victories, for patience learned through setbacks, for suggestions that help you stay on course, even for a smile from a stranger.

- *Pray for other people's dreams.* Ask God to help their dreams become reality. Praying for others helps us take the focus off our own world and shift it to the needs and concerns of others.

- *Pray for the dream to be done God's way, because that's always the best way.* Every morning as I get out of bed I slide down on my knees and pray my own adaptation of a hymn-prayer by Adelaide Pollard: "Have your own way, Lord. Have your own way. You are the potter, I am the clay. Mold me and make my dream after your will. While I am living this day, you will fulfill."[1] This simple prayer may help you launch each day as well.

- *Pray for an attitude that is filled with trust in God.* Trusting God with our dreams fills us with courage and confidence to move forward and to resist opposition, to refuse to give up under pressure and amid disappointment.

- *Pray for healthy relationships.* Relationships that are unhealthy block our creativity, imagination, innovation, and productivity. We become drained instead of inspired. Ask God for guidance in this area. Seek His insights and discernment and wisdom in any relationships that lack health or require special care and attention.

- *Pray for persistence.* The single greatest reason that good dreams fail is giving up before the dream is realized. Nothing significant is ever attained without perseverance. The dream's payoff comes from seeing it through, with God at your side.
- *Pray with enthusiasm and expectation.* Pray as if you believe God is listening to and answering your prayers, because He is.[2]

Are you praying your dreams every day? I encourage you to stop reading and start praying, right now, because God never stops listening and He is always ready to answer. The power source is available. Are you plugged in?

Dear God, thank You for my dreams. I give them back to You to make them all they can possibly be. Amen.

# TWENTY-THREE

# E-N-T-R-E-P-R-E-N-E-U-R-I-A-L

## Why You Need to Keep "Jumping Scared"— A Walt Kallestad Chapter

If you picked up this book with some skepticism over whether God actually calls us to entrepreneurial faith, we pray that you are now ready to seek a vision from God. We hope you will take steps today to immerse yourself in the risky business of following God in meeting needs in your community.

There will always be some who object to using a business term in connection with ministry. When you're challenged by those who argue that God can do His work perfectly well without all this entrepreneur talk, tell them that you're simply following the world's best entrepreneur, Jesus, who came to earth on the instructions of the first Entrepreneur in the universe, our Creator God. If people criticize you because you characterize yourself as an entrepreneurial pastor or an entrepreneurial committee chair or an entrepreneurial youth worker, just ask if they would also like to become an entrepreneur of faith. This world is needy and desperate, and in desperate need of those who practice entrepreneurial faith. We need a great many more of you, so invite others to join the adventure.

## THE MAKEUP OF AN ENTREPRENEUR

The psalmist knew God's mighty ways and was confident that God gives visions to His people so they can perform mighty acts. "With God's help," he wrote, "we will do mighty things" (Psalm 60:12).

Entrepreneurs are called to partner with God in doing mighty things. So, as we close this book, let's take one last look at the deeper meaning of entrepreneurial faith.

### Enthusiasm

A few years ago, I had a heart attack while jogging, and I had to be checked out thoroughly to find what had caused it. I ended up getting heart surgery, an unheard-of six-way bypass. But even after extensive surgery that should have addressed all the blockages, my heart still wasn't beating right. The doctors and nurses were doing everything they could think of to get my heart to beat in a normal fashion. Finally, they had to do a procedure that involved stopping my heart.

The doctors said, "Maybe we should use these paddles." You know, the kind that put a gazillion volts through you? You see them on the medical-emergency television shows. And my wife and my son asked, "Why don't you just do it to get the heartbeat back to normal?" I looked at them and said, "Yeah! That's easy for you to say!" Anything that happens to others is a minor procedure. But anything that happens to *you* qualifies for the "major" category.

Instead, the doctors were able to use a procedure with medicine to stop and then restart my heart. They had to do it a couple of times. But on the second attempt my heart was fully converted. I heard the nurses out by the monitors shout, "He's converted! He's converted!" And the nurses next to my bed were giving each other high-fives.

Wouldn't it be great in the church if we got that enthusiastic about a life that is transformed? It's time that we get enthusiastic in our churches. "Enthusiasm" is a good word to live by, because the literal meaning of the Greek phrase *en theos* is "full of God." Entrepreneurs need to be filled to overflowing with the love of God.

## Nurture New Ideas

New ideas are not always welcome, especially in churches. The seven last words of the dying church are "We've never done it that way before." Don't let the status quo hold you back. Think of ideas beyond your local congregation. Think about the community around you. And think globally.

We've had people give money to the Community Church of Joy because we were involved in the community. It didn't come from our members or even from casual attendees. In fact, we received a $2 million gift from a woman who was a Catholic, whom I had never met, and who never went to this church. She was 102 years old when she died. She had heard about what we were doing for kids. She had heard of our highly rated preschool. Our children's ministry was attracting kids from all over the region.

We also have a memorial garden that is open to all, no matter what their religious affiliation. We find that funerals are an especially critical time to show mercy and touch lives with the love of Christ, a time when people are most aware of their limits, their finiteness, and their need for something or Someone who is stronger than they are. We have ministered to the entire community through our memorial gardens.

We also have a far-reaching leadership center. If we discover something that is useful and effective, we love to share it. If you have something to share with us, we provide a platform. We are a teaching church that can multiply your discovery and send it out around the world. We coach pastors and their leadership teams, and our church sponsors several major conferences every year on topics from evangelism to entrepreneurship.

## Turn Failure Forward

Don't be afraid to fail. In fact, if you're an entrepreneur you *will* fail. I guarantee it. At Community Church of Joy, we had a vision for a major retirement resort. Phoenix is a popular destination for retirees from colder areas of the nation. We worked hard to turn this dream into reality. In fact, we even made an announcement that we were moving ahead to develop and sell homes on our forty-acre retirement center campus. We thought we were following God's lead in this, but guess what? We failed.

The market softened, and the developers realized that it was not the right time and place to sell life-care apartments. We were only able to sell half of the units when the developers, who risked their money, had to close down the project.

However, we are developing a new and improved version. If all goes as planned (and it won't), we'll break ground on a community park, in partnership with our city, along with mixed-use residential and commercial developments, within two years. We are developing an intergenerational community that will meet the original dream and the vision for that property.

Entrepreneurs turn failure into new opportunity.

## Reach Out with Humility

When you get so far out there that you're beyond anything you could afford or do on your own, it's pretty humbling. In fact, one of God's easiest jobs is to keep us humble. One of His toughest jobs is to make us believe we're worth something. When we fail, we feel worthless. But God doesn't want us to feel defeated; He only wants us to know a healthy humility.

Anything you see going on at the campus of Community Church of Joy isn't because of human hands. God has led us, and we've trusted God every step of the way.

I remember the time we saw the need to erect a tower on the southeast corner of our property, the edge of our campus that abuts an intersection of two busy thoroughfares. We formed a group to explore the feasibility of building the tower. We found out that erecting a tower that would serve the purposes of beckoning people to our church, that would add aesthetically to the area, and that would meet zoning and other requirements would cost approximately $750,000. With so many other needs in the community, we simply could not justify spending that much money on a tower.

Then our general manager, Wayne Skaff, contacted a local cellular company to explore their need for a microwave transmitting tower in our part of Phoenix. Within a few months, we had a beautiful tower at the corner of the church property, with a big cross on each side signaling to thousands of passersby that we were ready to be of service to them. And we didn't pay a dime for the tower.

## Expect the Best

Never settle for mediocrity. Move the benchmark higher than it is.

People throw worn furniture, torn clothing, and old canned goods at the church—expecting us to use their castoffs to meet the needs of the truly needy. God doesn't work that way. He doesn't ask for our leftovers. It's time to step up and say, "No, that's not what we're about. We serve the Creator of the universe, we can do things with excellence."

You need to set a standard of excellence. Not opulence, but excellence. In ministry, God deserves our best. And those in our communities deserve nothing less than our best. Remember, we serve others in the name of the Most High God.

## Pray Persistently

Prayer is the most powerful force in the world. And prayer works. For a compelling biblical model of a spiritual entrepreneur who understood the need for prayer, and who experienced the power of prayer, read the prayer of Solomon at the dedication of the Temple, recorded in 1 Kings 8.

The oppression of God's people broke God's heart. He saw His loved ones whipped and humiliated as slaves in Egypt. God searched for someone who could hear His voice, and Moses was listening. Although Moses had his qualms, he kept talking and listening to God. Through their continuous conversations, God instilled in Moses the courage and wisdom that he needed to lead God's people out of Egypt. Moses's greatest ability was his availability.

James declares, "You do not have, because you do not ask God. When you ask, you do not receive, because you ask with wrong motives, that you may spend what you get on your pleasures" (James 4:2-3, NIV). Make prayer a top priority, and when you pray, maintain your focus on others and their needs. There is no room for selfishness or ego in prayer.

## Risk Relentlessly

Mike Martz, head coach of the St. Louis Rams, once said, "Give me courage, Lord, to take risks. Not the ones that are expected, not the relatively safe risks, but those I could avoid. The go-for-broke ones."[1] Taking over the head-coaching duties in 2000 after Dick Vermeil retired from coaching the Rams, Martz led the team to the playoffs in each of his first two seasons as head coach, including a berth in Super Bowl XXXVI. In 2001, he became only the second coach in NFL history to lead a team to five consecutive wins after an 0–5 start. The Rams are the only franchise in NFL history to score at least five hundred points in three different seasons. Martz's team also produced three consecutive NFL most valuable players (in 1999, 2000, and 2001).[2]

Are you willing to lay it all on the line and go for broke? Are you willing to trust big, risk big, and suffer the consequences if things don't turn out like others expect?

Years ago, church growth specialist Lyle Schaller advised us, "When you relocate, its like walking on thin ice. You have no idea when it's going to give way."

That is exactly what it's like. You're walking across a frozen lake, and the temperature is hovering around thirty-two degrees. You hear cracking sounds off to the side. Then you feel the ice settling, and water starts running across the surface of the ice in the distance. You're still standing, but the ice is shifting and beginning to give way. When you live the life of a spiritual entrepreneur, it's never a safe feeling being out there. But by faith we choose to step out, and to remain there to obey God's call.

## Exploit Criticism

Learn from your critics. They usually don't mean to be helpful, but their input can make you sharper. When people tell you, "You're not really preaching the gospel" or "You're crazy to think we can accomplish such a thing," let it make you better. Let it help you study more, work harder, think more carefully and more thoroughly. Make sure you turn criticism into something positive.

## Nurture Change

The things that brought you to where you are today will not take you where you want to be tomorrow. Circumstances change. Needs change. The community changes. And you have to change.

We continually live in change. Change is resisted because it's uncomfortable. But an entrepreneurial ministry nurtures change.

## Evaluate Everything

Evaluate all pieces of information that you are given. Don't swallow it whole. Break it down into small bites before you swallow.

As well, evaluate yourself—your habits, your attitudes, your actions, your results, your perceptions. Are you allowing ego to enter into the equation and influence your decision making? Are you trying to accomplish something to please someone else—anyone other than God? Are you trying to prove something? Ask yourself the hard questions, and don't accept evasive or incomplete answers. Ask God to reveal and make clear what is in your heart, since often we are blind to our own mixed motives.

We just went through a 360-degree evaluation, where members of our staff were evaluated not just by their supervisors but also by their peers and those they supervise. This gave us a much clearer picture of each person's true impact, as seen by others close to us. In the church it's tough, because we don't want to hurt anybody. We've bought into a myth. We've concluded that because God has made everyone wonderful, we have to let people lead music, for instance, who have no talent and little musical ability. In truth, we allow this to continue because we don't want to enter the difficult area of evaluation, which might lead to disappointment but in the long term leads to people being placed where their gifts can be exercised more fully. Evaluation can help you identify a person who is talented, but perhaps not in the position where he or she is currently serving. Evaluating your staff allows you to make some moves that will put everyone in positions where God can use their strengths to the best advantage.

Football coach Bob Stoops won a national championship at the University of Oklahoma in just his second year in the job. For the most part, these were players who were recruited by the university's previous coach. But Stoops evaluated each player and found that many weren't playing the position for which they were best suited. By switching players to where they were at their best, Stoops once again turned OU into champions.

### Unleash a Servant's Heart

You can't develop entrepreneurial faith if you're seeking your own profit. In all we do, we must be looking for the good of others. This is the heart of a servant. It is the heart of Jesus, the world's foremost Entrepreneur.

Entrepreneurs possess a high degree of confidence. They are task oriented and tenacious. They are single-minded and sometimes might be accused of having tunnel vision. But these traits contribute to perseverance and endurance, which are necessary to bring visions into reality. However, when your driven nature begins to seek glory or advancement or plaudits for yourself, ego is kicking in. It will shove you off track and dim your vision. Always remember: We live as spiritual entrepreneurs to serve others, not ourselves.

## Remember God's Promises and God's Protection

It's so easy to forget about God.

A little girl wanted to go see her new baby sister in the hospital. Her parents let her walk into the room. When she saw her baby sister lying in the crib, she got right up to the infant's face and said, "Baby, tell me what God is like. I'm already starting to forget."

We're too busy, too tired, too burdened, too stretched. We work so hard that it's easy to start believing that *we're* responsible for any successes we're a part of. We forget God.

Don't forget God. I use a one-year Bible and try to spend an hour each day praying. This helps me stay focused on the priority of my relationship with my Father.

## Innovate with Passion and Persistence

If you're trying to make a change in a product or service, yet lack passion and persistence, you will soon quit. Live your passion. Stick to it. Life is too short to play it safe.

I once was asked, "What would you be willing to exchange your life for?" I realized later that how I answered the question uncovered the passion that lay deep within my heart.

## Aim at the Target

Do you know what you are aiming for? Can you tell others what your target is? You've got to set out clear goals and objectives. You've got to write out your values, your mission statement, and your strategies. And don't make the documents so thick that no one will take the time to read them. Summarize the big idea into a clear, descriptive statement. Bullet point the heart of the vision. Capture the dream and summarize it in just a sentence or two.

## Leap Scared

This point comes last only because it begins with the letter L. But it certainly is not the least important aspect of entrepreneurial faith.

When Michelle, our church's missions director, was a little girl, she lived for the day she could go off the high dive at the local swimming pool. Finally she was old enough and her mother said, "Okay, you can climb the ladder and jump off the diving board." Michelle got up there, walked out to the edge, and looked over into the air and water below. She was paralyzed with anxiety. She never dreamed the diving board was that high above the surface of the water. Totally humiliated, totally embarrassed, she slowly walked back and climbed down the ladder.

Later, she worked up enough courage to try again. She went up the ladder, and as she stood at the end of the diving board a little boy behind her said, "You know what? If you can't jump brave, jump scared!" So she took the leap. She loved it, ran back to the ladder, and jumped again and again.

As we take every step, we are jumping scared. The critics raise their voices. The enemy fills our minds with doubts. Friends switch sides and join the chorus of negativity. We hear the ice cracking and see the gap widening and wonder just how long it will be before we slip beneath the surface.

But in spite of it all, we go ahead and take the next step. We're jumping scared. And when we do, we're leaping into the arms of the God who will never let us fall.

You're living the life of entrepreneurial faith. Go ahead and jump scared. But as you do, jump with faith.

# THE ENTREPRENEUR'S COMMISSION

There's a good reason why we call this the life of entrepreneurial faith. It's because even the grandest vision won't work without faith.

God knows the end from the beginning, but we don't. He gives us a vision, but usually just enough for us to get started, to take the first step. Then He gives more insight and direction, some contacts, a like-minded partner, a team—but just enough help so that we can take the next step. God knows the outcome already, but all we see is what's in front of us. And even that view can be cloudy.

In launching and leading bold initiatives to expand the Kingdom of God on earth, we have no need greater than faith in God. We follow a big God who gives us a big vision, but we also encounter big adversity and opposition and heartache. Through it all, God is faithful to lead as long as we are faithful to follow. And following Him requires faith.

So at the end of this book, as we encourage you to embrace all the joys and challenges of entrepreneurial faith, let us leave you with a prayer. This is our commission to you and our benediction as you follow God's call in turning the vision He gives into reality.

> As you go, may our loving Lord go before you to show you the way,
> Behind you to encourage you,
> Beside you to be your best Friend,
> Above you to watch over you.
> And may He be in your heart
> Filling you with His peace, power, perseverance
> And His uncontainable joy.
> *Amen!*

# THE OPPORTUNITY-SCREENING PROCESS

## Getting Smarter About Taking Risks

C an you think of a project or initiative that you launched with great optimism and confidence, but it only led you down a path of disappointment? A great new ministry that was tailor-made to meet needs, but no one showed up? A fundraising campaign that barely covered the consultant's fee? A building project that ran *way* over budget? A new outreach that completely bombed?

As we've stated more than once, the life of entrepreneurial faith is a life of risk. If you aren't prepared for disappointment, then you're not ready for entrepreneurial faith.

But that doesn't mean we have to invite disappointment by being stupid about risk. While spiritual entrepreneurship demands that we take risks— sometimes big ones—God wants us to be smart about the risks we're taking. Entrepreneurs of faith are constantly aware of the changes taking place around them. They size up an opportunity and then seize it for God's glory. Identifying changes that in turn trigger opportunities is at the heart of the opportunity-screening process. In this process, the successful entrepreneur distinguishes between a good idea and a true opportunity.

## WILL THE TRUE OPPORTUNITY PLEASE STAND UP?

Entrepreneurs tend to be creative people—full of ideas and quick to come up with options and alternatives to what already exists. But an idea is not the same as an opportunity. Good ideas might be just that—things worth pondering, things that spur more thinking, or things that are interesting subjects for discussion—but nothing more. No matter how fresh or creative or radical the idea, it's not necessarily an opportunity.

Opportunity implies there's a true need or demand for which the idea provides an answer or solution. This is how Jeffry Timmons defines an entrepreneurial opportunity: "An opportunity has the qualities of being attractive, durable, and timely and is anchored in [a] product or service which creates or adds value for its buyer or end user."[1] Discerning the extent of the value that is created captures the essence of the opportunity-screening process.

For a business venture, opportunity screening is expressed largely in financial terms: What's the profit margin, and how much wealth will be created? But for a church-related venture, as with other nonprofits, an opportunity may or may not reflect financial value, but it always reflects the missional purpose of the organization to create social and/or spiritual value. Further, it meets the true felt need of the end user. Therefore, the action of creating or adding value for a church-related venture involves meeting a clearly demonstrated need while fulfilling the intended mission of the church. Those two requirements guide us in the opportunity-screening process.

Subjecting our ideas—even the very best ideas—to this process makes us smarter about the risks we take. And it protects us and our ministries from the fallout of unwise risk taking. When we take an unwise risk and our project or ministry bombs, we have to deal with the debris that is left behind:

- We can lose our credibility.
- We can lose a lot of money.
- We can lose support.
- We can waste a lot of time.

## FEASIBILITY STUDIES

Doing a feasibility study can reduce your risk and help you hit your target as you develop new ministries, programs, and community outreaches. A feasibility study asks the question "Can it be done?" And if so, "How can it best be done?" Doing a study does not indicate a lack of faith, only the presence of wisdom. In the New Testament, Jesus invites us to test the waters before plunging in:

> Suppose one of you wants to build a tower. Will he not first sit down
> and estimate the cost to see if he has enough money to complete it?
> For if he lays the foundation and is not able to finish it, everyone who
> sees it will ridicule him, saying, "This fellow began to build and was
> not able to finish." (Luke 14:28-30, NIV)

A feasibility study can be your process of modeling a project before you commit to it. You model not with clay but with a picture that includes the conceptual, marketing, organizational, and financial aspects of your vision. One of our visions at the Community Church of Joy is to develop an aquatics center for our community. A local swim club enthusiastically joined in our vision. We imagined that there was enough need in our community to build and sustain the center. But instead of jumping into the water right away, we decided to first stick our toe in, to see if the project was feasible.

Through the help of a friend, we enlisted an economic planner who had conducted the economic analysis for Disneyland. He gave us a report we didn't want to see. According to his model, the aquatics center could sustain itself only if we could find donated funds to build it. With this news we put the project on temporary hold. Disappointing? Yes. But much less costly than discovering that we had poured the cement for the pool yet couldn't finish it.

A well-done feasibility study can reduce your risk, help you live in the future before you actually get there, help you count the cost before you venture out too far, allow you to anticipate the key questions, and pave the way for your ministry plan by doing most of the necessary research up front. Think about a project or new program you would like to launch, and consider how a feasibility study can help you.

## THE COMPONENTS OF A FEASIBILITY STUDY

Here are five steps that will help you obtain the greatest benefit from a feasibility study.

### 1. Discovering the Need

The first step is listening to your community, your constituents, your competition, and your Creator. As you observe, you reach the point of saying, "There's a need here! And this is an opportunity that fits with our mission and vision." Like pieces of a puzzle, the needs and the resources start to fit together. You may need to conduct lots of informal exploration and discovery, especially if there isn't much in your pocketbook. In fact, we've found an underabundance of funds to be helpful, as it keeps us lean and forces us to think more creatively. This process is also rooted in prayer, as you allow God to nurture a passion in your heart.

### 2. Defining the Dream

As the dream takes shape, you can begin to define the feasibility process: Put it on paper, in a few short paragraphs. What does the project look like at this time, conceptually and in broad-strokes terms—not with all the details. What is the picture from ten thousand feet? If you had just three minutes to explain your dream to another person, what would you say?

As you summarize the project to capture its essence, consider:

- Who do we want to serve?
- How do we want to organize it?
- What might it cost from what we know now, and how will we pay for it?
- What other questions do we want to answer?

These questions form the outline of the feasibility study.

## 3. Discerning the Competition

This phase can be formal or informal. In the marketing world, it's called a market analysis or industry analysis. Basically, regarding the need you plan to meet, how are others already meeting that need? Through an industry analysis, you benchmark existing models and competition. You may have to find new data or there may be some statistics available from studies that have already been done.

Once you gather all the needed data, the results will help you confirm or adjust your assumptions. For example: In designing our plan to build a recording studio, we adjusted the rates that we would charge for recording sessions based on what other studios in the area were charging.

## 4. Drafting the Model

Once you have a fairly clear picture of the current needs and the existing competition for meeting those needs, you can begin to create your model accordingly. To do this, you first define or redefine the questions first posed in your outline in step 2. What do you truly want to know? Then, based upon your research, write out your answers. You can now set up realistic financial assumptions, based upon the projections. From this you can create a model budget.

## 5. Determining the Results

The final step is to ask, "What do our answers tell us?" By interpreting the results, you have gained a clearer picture of your future. With our aquatics center, we concluded that we could not service the debt with revenues generated from operations.

There is a range of types of feasibility studies, from highly informal (talking with some friends) to highly formal (a complete market study). The informal studies serve best when high certainty is not needed. Formal studies cost more, but they may be worth the cost if you want to avoid a negative experience. You can make these studies less costly to you by asking potential partners to help underwrite the research. Or you might find a research grant or individual gift to support a formal study.

## How to Reduce Your Risk

Most entrepreneurial researchers agree that at least half of all new ventures fail in the first two years. That's the bad news. The good news is that there are reasons for this; and if you pay attention to the following areas, your chances of success will increase dramatically. Here are three major reasons for failure.

### Neglecting Strategic Issues

You can't keep your finger on everything, but you'd better keep it on the strategic issues. Strategic issues can either minimize your risk or they can doom your venture to failure. These issues include: understanding your marketing niche or approach, grasping the supplier or customer economic relationships, guarding against any diversification into unrelated businesses, being careful not to confuse "great ideas" with true opportunities, never tackling a big project without analyzing the cash-flow implications, and doing sufficient contingency planning. Unfortunately, the management team is often so close to a new venture's trees that it does not perceive the forest—the strategic flaw.

You can avoid strategic miscues by (a) frequently reviewing the principles of entrepreneurial leadership; (b) welcoming an outside consultant, board member, or mentor to observe the organization and candidly comment on potential causes of trouble or failure; (c) benchmarking against other similar ventures; (d) developing key indicators so that downward trends can be caught and analyzed immediately; (e) filtering new opportunities through the lens of the mission and strategic plan; and (f) attacking "soft spots" regularly through a discipline of focusing upon one strategic area each month (for example: contingency plans, market niche, and so on).

## Management Problems

General management problems are a second primary cause of failure, but such problems are difficult to detect if the entrepreneur is also the manager, especially if he or she is unwilling to let go of control. The management team's competency may not have kept up with the pace of the organization's growth. The financial manager in particular may not measure up to the size and growth of the organization. Also, turnover may leave huge gaps in knowledge, or the team may be trying to operate financially like a big company rather than a lean enterprise.

An innovative entrepreneur can avoid this cause of failure by immediately and continually grooming an entrepreneurial team with talents beyond those of the founder. These may include paid staff, board members, consultants, volunteers, and outsourced vendors.

## Inadequate Financial Planning

When the mission, vision, and values are clear, the key leader has the flexibility to resource and structure the economics of the venture in a variety of ways. And many of these approaches can decrease the cash-flow risk. Most important, the entrepreneur can't let the financial management and strategic thinking get away from him or her.

Poor planning and inadequate financial and accounting systems, practices, and controls can lead to a venture's collapse, even if it is otherwise flourishing. If the financial controls are weak, the venture can move through cash fast enough to make you dizzy. This can be the result of poor pricing, overextending credit, excessive debt, inadequate cash projections, poor reporting to management, miscosting, or not understanding the fixed and variable costs.

If you see trouble brewing, or if staff members, board members, or others in positions to spot potential problems bring things to your attention, take immediate action. If you avoid assessing and addressing the real issues, it will only accelerate the downward spiral. Employees may see trouble brewing early on, which will be reflected in lower morale or lower productivity. Investors, lenders, and trade creditors will see signs of trouble if they have access to financial statements or notice increasing delinquency in payments.

To help you gain a clearer understanding of the problem or problems, begin by assessing the clarity of your venture's mission. Analyze the management team and the venture's strategic posture and direction. And take a hard look at the financial numbers, particularly an analysis of the cash flow and position.

Once the key issues are identified, the diagnostic team can dig deeper to discover underlying issues and develop strategic solutions.

# A SAMPLE STRATEGIC PLAN

## Getting the Most Important Components Down on Paper

usiness ventures build success upon the clear analysis of a business plan. The business plan serves two purposes. First, it helps the entrepreneur carefully think through the key strategic issues that will increase the chances for success of the venture. Second, the plan becomes the tool that invites key investors and other partners to invest financially in the venture.

Entrepreneurial ministries and enterprises also benefit from a strategic plan. A strategic plan shares many similarities with a business plan, but with more emphasis on the mission and program components and somewhat less on the marketing and financial components. This is not to say that understanding the market and finances is not as important, but less detail may be given to those areas in a strategic plan.

Strategic planning for most church-based ventures assumes that the *mission,* rather than financial profitability, drives the process. If, however, profitability cannot be achieved through the proposed operations, either philanthropic funds need to be secured or the feasibility of the venture should be reconsidered.

Strategic plans for church enterprises also differ from pure business plans in terms of who develops the plan. Whereas an individual entrepreneur can develop a business plan, churches and other nonprofit organizations need to gain the consensus of a wider circle of key stakeholders. This may consist of board members or other key volunteer leaders. The strategic plan can be developed through successive iterations, as input is gained from the key leader, a core planning team, key stakeholders, and finally the broader constituency. As stakeholders offer their input and provide reactions to drafts of the plan, not only does the plan improve, but the organization and the program also gain a broader ownership and support.

The type of plan you develop ultimately will depend on its intended audience. If the church is seeking a mortgage or line of credit, the plan will need to be adapted to the financial perspectives of the lenders. If it supports a fundraising campaign, the donors' interests will be considered first. If it becomes the plan for operating a new venture, more detailed strategies and action steps will be included.

The strategic plan for a new venture at the Community Church of Joy in Phoenix is included here as an example. It includes a *concept paper,* an *operations plan,* and a *funding proposal* all for the same project. We encourage you to find ways to adapt these ideas to help you make concrete plans for developing the dream God has placed in your heart.

## CONCEPT PAPER FOR THE CROSSING

The Crossing is a positive place for teenagers to celebrate friendship with one another and to connect with God. It will attract teens in the community through entertainment, sports, and food, to an exciting venue that will create a contagious atmosphere. Through the acceptance by peers and guidance of young-adult mentors, The Crossing will support teens on their journey to become dynamic servant-leaders in their communities and in the world.

## Overview

Today's teenagers carry in their hearts the hope for our churches, our communities, and our world. If they thrive, all of us will thrive. If they grow into the healthy and compassionate adults that God dreams for them to become, then our dreams for them will have been fulfilled.

Unfortunately, many teens are not thriving. A recent study published in the *Sourcebook of Criminal Justice Statistics* indicates that serious teenage juvenile behavior affects a large number of American teenagers. Of particular concern is the number of children who are becoming involved in serious criminal activity as a result of poor peer-group relationships and a distancing from family. Teens involved in unwholesome activities cross socioeconomic boundaries and impact all cities, regardless of size. Teens in our community are as at risk as any in our nation.

Although individual efforts by some communities and agencies are designed to address these concerns, few provide the preventative solution of a safe environment in which teens are attracted to activities by positive peer-group interaction. The Crossing, located on the Community Church of Joy campus, proposes to address this need by implementing and developing Arizona's first faith-based club for teens and their families. The Crossing will also serve as a prototype for other communities across the country that seek to offer hope for their youth. The Crossing is seeking support for construction, program development, and program dissemination to other communities that wish to address teen problems in an innovative, safe, and proactive environment.

Why do we need The Crossing? Here are just a few reasons:

- *Our teens are everywhere among us.* Some thirty thousand teenagers live within five miles of the Community Church of Joy campus.

- *Our teens are not safe.* Thirty-one percent of teenagers reported being hit or beaten by someone their own age, and another nineteen percent were assaulted by an older teen. Twenty-nine percent reported being victims of a racial or ethnic insult, and twelve percent reported being attacked by a gang.[1]
- *Our teens are not supervised.* Teenagers are faced with ever-increasing amounts of unsupervised time, as a result of single working parents and families where both father and mother are working to support the household.
- *Our teens are getting into trouble at alarming rates.* Newfound freedom, resulting from decreased parental supervision at home, opens a window of opportunity for teens to become involved in substance abuse and increased sexual activity.
- *Our teens have no place to go.* Teenagers claim they have no safe place to hang out with friends, other than the mall or movie theater.
- *Our current teen facility is overcrowded.* With large numbers of teens involved on a weekly basis, The Bridge has run out of space. We can't allow teens to be turned away and miss the greatest opportunity of their lives to connect with Christ and this caring community.

The crisis among our teenagers will only grow. If something is not done now, the problems among teens will accelerate. In the past decade, Arizona's growth-rate percentage was exceeded nationally only by the state of Nevada, although Arizona's growth by total population was higher. The number of teens in our community and the resulting challenges they face will only increase in the years ahead.

## Who Will The Crossing Serve?

Primary audience: twelve- to nineteen-year-olds within metropolitan Phoenix who live within a twenty-five-mile radius of The Crossing.

Secondary audiences: teens throughout the Phoenix metropolitan area and parents of teenagers who participate in Crossing programs.

National audiences: young adults who want to develop leadership skills as interns at The Crossing, serving teens and their families. Also, leaders across the country who are searching for a high-impact model to use in reaching teenagers in their community.

## How Will The Crossing Help Teens and Families?

The Crossing will connect youth and families in our community to God, one another, and a network of supportive mentors, resulting in healthier, faith-filled teens and more productive citizens in our community.

## Distinct Features of The Crossing

- The Crossing will offer teens a safe, positive place to go for fun and friendship.
- The Crossing will bring the whole family back together. In a world that pulls families apart, this place will help teens and their families build bonds of love, creating memories that will last a lifetime.
- The Crossing will build people through people. The strength of The Crossing will be its team of caring young adults and parents who invest themselves in serving and mentoring youth.
- The Crossing will help fulfill the mission of the Community Church of Joy: "that all may know Jesus Christ and become his empowered followers." Our community is exploding with youth who are searching for spiritual meaning and relational connection, and The Crossing will meet this need.

## What Will Happen at The Crossing?

### Serving Teens in the Community

The Crossing will give hope to the thirty thousand–plus teenagers in our community through concerts, extreme sports, worship, Bible study, after-school activities, small groups, and leadership training.

*Serving Families*

Through the teenagers, The Crossing will also serve the multitude of families in our community. They will participate in concerts, parent support, sports events, and many other family-building activities.

*Serving Joy Community School*

The Crossing will provide the students of Joy Community School (K-12) with a common-area facility for the middle school and future high school, where lunches can be served and students can interact between classes. Classroom facilities will be adjacent to The Crossing.

## What Will The Crossing Facility Include?

- The Crossing will welcome teens and their families into a large, high-energy, warehouse-type space that can be customized to the needs and trends of the current teen culture.
- Teens will have a place of their own that is a home away from home to meet friends, talk about their faith, and have fun together.
- The Crossing will include teen-friendly amenities with video games, pool and foosball tables, a snack bar, and soft, comfortable furniture.
- Wednesday nights and weekends will be ignited with great concerts, worship, learning, and meeting new friends.
- The Crossing will include a stage, flexible seating space for about six hundred (theater style), high-tech lighting and sound, a food service area, and offices.
- Approximate interior size: ten thousand square feet.

## What Investment Will It Take to Build The Crossing?

The cost for construction will be approximately [dollar amount], of which [dollar amount] has already been committed. This will complete the structure, hardscaping, landscaping, and technology. An additional [dollar amount] in advance gifts is needed to move forward and fulfill this dream for youth and their families. In order to reduce construction costs, volunteers will be invited to help finish some of the facility's interior (for example: staging, cabinets, and so on) through donations of time and materials.

## How Will The Crossing Be Sustained Financially?

The Crossing facilities will be developed through the generous support of friends of the Community Church of Joy who believe in the vision to reach the youth and families of our community. Funds for ongoing operation of The Crossing will be provided in several ways, including:

- allocations from the Community Church of Joy's general fund for use by Teen, Youth, and Family Ministry, and other regular ministry uses, as is currently being done
- allocations from Joy Community School's budget for use of space during school hours
- space rental fees for special events, such as birthday parties and other group events
- food-service fees from snack bar and gift shop sales
- special gifts and an endowment fund for ongoing support

## How Can Individuals Help?

Individuals can support the development of The Crossing with a one-time gift or a pledge that is fulfilled on a weekly, monthly, or annual basis. Currently, commitments are being sought for gifts of cash, stock, bequests, or other assets in the range of [dollar amount]. Gifts or commitments of any size will be most gratefully welcomed.

Gifts can be committed to The Crossing by completing a Crossing Commitment Card or by contacting The Joy Foundation. All gifts are tax deductible.

## Information About the Sponsoring Organization

The Community Church of Joy is a community-oriented, faith-based organization that has enjoyed unprecedented success in its twenty-five year history. With more than twelve thousand constituents, this community stands poised to develop new programs and activities that will not only benefit its community, but which will also serve as a model of success to be adapted by other communities across the nation.

The Community Church of Joy is committed to doing whatever it takes to build a community that reaches out to new people and helps them grow, by affirming and upholding the God-given worth of each individual. From this commitment comes a sincere desire to help people foster, build, and experience dynamic, vital relationships with one another. This commitment to people has resulted in the Community Church of Joy's establishing a successful preschool, K-8 school, school of performing arts, leadership-training programs presented across the nation, and the development of a Leadership Center on the Community Church of Joy campus. As an organization dedicated to needs-based solutions for real-people problems, the Community Church of Joy will implement and develop The Crossing to respond to the needs of teenagers in the Phoenix metropolitan community. The Crossing will respond to research that identified an emerging regional and national need for a new and innovative approach to attract teens to a safe, positive environment for peer and adult-mentor interaction.

## Phase I of the Master Plan for Families

The Crossing is the first step in an exciting master-planned activity area for families in our community. In a world that pulls families apart, the campus of the Community Church of Joy will help families build bonds of faith and love, creating memories that last a lifetime.

## The Joy Pavilion and Park

At the heart of Joy's campus, children and adults will be captivated by this beautiful park setting where they can enjoy friends, relax, or burn off some energy. Younger children will enjoy climbing, playing, and interacting with their parents and friends.

The park will include the following:

- A pavilion will provide shade for as many as 250 persons who can use the space for picnics, receptions, banquets, and other food service.
- A courtyard is a central gathering place and walkway with colorful flower gardens, trees, park benches, picnic areas, and grassy lawns.
- An outdoor chapel will host outdoor worship, weddings, and sing-alongs in a beautiful garden setting with an outdoor stage for music and drama.
- A playground will inspire family fun with interactive, age-graded playground equipment, with some special water-play features.
- Sports courts will support basketball, tennis, racquetball, and volleyball.
- Recreation fields will include soccer, softball, baseball, and football areas.

Approximate cost: [dollar amount]

## The Kid Kountry Clubhouse

On the south end of Joy Park, younger children and preteens will step into a world just right for kids, the Kid Kountry Clubhouse. This gathering place will capture the imagination of kids, as they sing, celebrate, and learn together on Sunday mornings, Wednesday nights, and at other times through special kid concerts and fun.

The Kid Kountry Clubhouse will include the following:

- A stage, flexible seating space for about five hundred (theater style), lighting, and sound. The larger space can be subdivided for smaller gatherings of fifty to two hundred. Approximate size: eight thousand square feet.

- A party room will welcome indoor picnics, family reunions, birthday parties, and other family celebrations. Approximate size: ten thousand square feet.

Approximate cost: [dollar amount]

## The Gym

Youth and families will enjoy informal recreation on evenings and weekends. This will be a great place to escape the summer heat for some exercise and fun.

Adjacent to The Crossing, the Gym will serve the following people and programs:

- Sports programs for youth and teenagers will be offered after school and on weekends, including basketball, volleyball, indoor soccer, gymnastics, and dance.
- Joy Community School's physical education and indoor sports programs will utilize this facility during school hours.
- Youth and adults also can get in shape at the Fitness Center.
- The Gym will include a full-length basketball court, bleachers for games, locker rooms, showers, stage, and a fitness center with workout/weight room.
- Approximate size: ten thousand square feet.

Approximate cost: [dollar amount]

# A SAMPLE OPERATIONS PLAN

## Getting the Details Down on Paper

### TABLE OF CONTENTS

## Executive Summary

Teenagers in the Phoenix metropolitan area, much like teens throughout the nation, are searching for a high-quality, imaginative, and highly relational home away from home. While their families are their number one priority, they also need an exciting place to meet friends, build friendships, and discover values that can help them through the whitewaters of personal and societal change. The Crossing will meet this need.

The Crossing will be a safe, positive place for youth to celebrate friendships and connect with God. Thousands of teens will be attracted to The Crossing through entertainment, sports, food, and, most of all, the contagious faith and acceptance of peers and young-adult mentors. The Crossing will also support hurting teens and their families in their darkest hours of deepest need. Ultimately, The Crossing will support teens on their journey to resist the destructive pressures around them and become dynamic servant-leaders in their world.

The Crossing, located on the campus of the Community Church of Joy, will be funded through community and church gifts and grants. Phase I of the facilities will include a teen club and outdoor amenities for teen entertainment and recreation, along with a prayer tower. Phase II will expand into a full-court indoor gymnasium, classrooms, offices, and expanded technology that can also expand the array of need-meeting programs.

The Crossing will serve teenagers through quality facilities, programs, and services. It will be formed as an Arizona nonprofit organization with its own board of directors, empowered by the board of the Joy Company and Community Church of Joy, a congregation of the Evangelical Lutheran Church in America. Its operational budget will be partially supported by income from programs, services, and products offered to teens and their families. The operating costs in the first five years will range from [dollar amount] during the first year of operation to [dollar amount] in Year Five. Program fees will grow to supply as much as 50 percent of the operating budget. Therefore, The Crossing will also depend upon gifts, grants, and an endowment fund to sustain its outreach.

The Crossing will create a significant positive impact in its community. Its staff and volunteers will serve more than [number] teen participants annually by [year] and more than [number] annually by [year]. Teens will receive support and assistance to strengthen their faith and values, while enhancing their connections with family, friends, and their community.

This Operations Plan provides the leaders of The Crossing with a broad framework for further development. As the vision for The Crossing unfolds, staff and leaders will continually refine and adapt this plan to the changing environment and needs of teenagers and their families.

## OUR MISSION, VISION, AND VALUES

The mission of The Crossing is this: The Crossing is a place where teenagers cross from fear to faith, from despair to hope, and from loneliness to love, through the power of God.

Our vision for The Crossing is to provide a safe, positive place for youth to celebrate friendships with one another and connect with God. Teens in our community will be attracted to The Crossing through entertainment, sports, food, and, most of all, the contagious faith and acceptance of peers and young-adult mentors. The Crossing supports teens on their journey of faith to become dynamic servant-leaders in their world.

Our values are both essential and far-reaching. They include outreach, transformation, hospitality, a positive "vibe," relational values, empowered volunteers, teen leadership, quality, integrity, safety, diversity, and character-based development as the core guiding values.

### Outreach

The Crossing will seek intentional and creative ways to connect with teens in the broader community.

## Transformation
Centered in God's love, The Crossing will intentionally help teenagers experience the life-transforming power of faith in every area of their lives.

## Hospitality
The Crossing will welcome both newcomers and active participants with open arms and acceptance in a nonthreatening atmosphere.

## A Positive "Vibe"
The Crossing will have a positive vibe through lighting, color, sound, music, and, most important, the positive attitude of the staff.

## Relational Values
Programs and facilities will serve as doorways to relationships, with a high ratio of paid/volunteer staff to participants who will "hang out" with the teens.

## Empowered Volunteers
Empowered, equipped volunteers who passionately love teens will express this love in genuinely winsome ways through their words and actions.

## Teen Leadership
The leadership potential of all teenagers will be encouraged and nurtured, as they help guide the direction for The Crossing.

## Quality
The programs, services, food, and facilities of The Crossing will reflect the high quality that attracts teens and encourages them to invite their friends.

## Integrity
The staff and volunteers of The Crossing will integrate high ethical values with their everyday decisions and actions.

## Safety
Teens and their parents will be confident that The Crossing provides a safe, secure environment, free from drugs, alcohol, sexual activity, and violence.

## Diversity
The Crossing will connect with the wide variety of interests and needs of teenagers from all walks of life.

## Character-Based Development
The staff will personally model and equip teens in the values and skills of character-based leadership, centered in faith and values.

## Who We Serve

Primary audience: twelve- to nineteen-year-olds who live within a twenty-five-mile radius of The Crossing.

Secondary audiences: teenagers throughout the Phoenix metropolitan area, as well as parents of teens who participate in Crossing programs.

National audiences: young adults who want to develop leadership skills in working with teens and their families. Also, leaders across the country who are searching for a high-impact model to reach teens in their communities.

## Goals, Objectives, and Strategies

### Goal I: To attract a multitude of teens to The Crossing.
Our objective includes drawing the following numbers of teenagers:
* [number] teen participants per year by [year]

To achieve this objective, we will pursue the following strategies:
* momentum-building events that encourage teens to invite friends
* need-meeting programs
* dynamic staff who build one-to-one relationships with teens

- ongoing community marketing/PR, targeting teens and their parents
- developing a first-class facility and amenities that will attract large numbers of teenagers

## Goal II: To care for the spiritual, emotional, mental, and physical needs of teenagers.

Our objectives include providing specific services and ministries to the following numbers of teenagers:

- [number] teens to receive personal care/mentoring each year by [year]
- [number] teen participants per year will report reduced personal, negative, or substance-abuse activities by [year]

To achieve these objectives, we will pursue the following strategies:

- programs that inspire and assist teens in the development of their whole lives—faith, intellect, physical fitness, relationships, and personal well-being
- strategic alliances with the overall mission of the Community Church of Joy and other dynamic teen-based service organizations
- intervention for teens in need

## Goal III: To invite teenagers to a relationship with God and the faith community.

Our objectives include the following outcomes and ministries:

- [number] teenagers per year to express new faith foundations through a Crossing program by [year]
- [number] teens per year to report new involvement in a faith community by [year]

To achieve these objectives, we will pursue the following strategies:

- introduction to faith, which will be integrated into ongoing programs and events

- intentional assimilation of teenagers and their families into the broader life of area churches

## Goal IV: To support healthy relationships between teens and their family members, their peers, and their community.

Our objectives include the following outcomes and ministries:

- [number] parents per year to participate in Crossing programs by [year]
- [number] teenagers and parents to report improved relationships in their families through programs of The Crossing by [year]
- [number] teens to report improved relationships with peers through programs of The Crossing by [year]

To achieve these objectives, we will pursue the following strategies:

- parent-teen relationship-building programs and activities
- parent involvement in leadership and service for Crossing programs
- peer relationship building as part of ongoing programs

## Goal V: To equip teenagers to become lifelong learners and servant-leaders.

Our objectives include the following outcomes and ministries:

- [number] teens participating in some type of spiritual growth/service activity by [year]
- [number] teens per year to report involvement in some type of leadership role by [year]

To achieve these objectives, we will pursue the following strategies:

- high-energy, relational learning environments, such as small groups, classes, and large-group presentations, utilizing many forms of media and art
- leadership-training track
- process for helping teens explore their personal passion and gifts

## Goal VI: The Crossing organization will positively impact its local, regional, and national communities.

Our objectives include the following outcomes and ministries:

- [number] schools or community groups to be served each year with quality, character-based substance-abuse and sexuality-awareness seminars by [year]
- [number] local teens each year to be equipped with job and leadership skills so they can positively contribute to society in their current and future careers by [year]
- Crossing volunteers to assist in [number] major community-improvement activities each year by [year]
- [number] financially challenged teenagers and their families to be served by The Crossing staff and volunteers each year by [year]
- [number] organizations across the country to receive assistance from The Crossing each year in their own community outreaches to teenagers by [year]

To achieve these objectives, we will pursue the following strategies:

- substance-abuse-awareness assemblies in local schools and community seminars at The Crossing
- sexuality-awareness assemblies in local schools and community seminars at The Crossing
- job fairs and career-development seminars at The Crossing
- special programs to adopt/assist needy families that include teenage members
- annual community-improvement project (for example: park cleanup)
- collaboration with other teen-oriented, community-service organizations
- materials, Web sites, consulting, and other resources to assist other churches and community organizations in visioning and developing their outreach to teenagers

## PROGRAM PLAN AND FEES

## Program Components

### *CrossOver: Phase I, [time estimate]*

This is a wide-open door where teens can come in and "cross over" from the world into an atmosphere of celebration, grace, acceptance, and unconditional love. The staff (both paid and volunteer) will seek to build relationships in order to earn the right to be heard by teenagers.

The Crossing Club is the central place that embraces teens and meets their broad social, recreational, and entertainment needs. Through music, videos, pool tables, interactive video games, a place to hang out, and great food, teens invite their friends into this clubhouse environment. Well-trained staff will ensure a safe environment and will reach out to those who attend with love and friendship rather than just policing the area as "chaperones." There will be concerts, dances, theater presentations, battle-of-the-band nights, and more. Whatever is on the edge and attracts teens in a wholesome way will be considered.

Another important component will be performing arts and visual arts. Not only will the arts serve as an integral part of the presentations for teens, but teenagers also will perform and tour with the traveling music and drama teams. Opportunities for multiple expressions of the visual arts also will be incorporated into the program.

Special off-site events will include trips to California theme parks and amusement parks, overnight trips, ski trips, mission and service projects, and other events, all providing great opportunities for active youth to invite their friends.

Seminars, classes, and workshops will focus on faith issues and practical-living topics.

Crisis help and counseling will provide a safe place and support for at-risk teens. Teenagers will be assisted by caring professionals to discover or sustain a positive, drug-free life.

The Crossing interns will develop a high-energy "character-development" themed program for presentation two days each week in public schools. These assemblies are funded by a government grant. They will give tremendous exposure to The Crossing and its staff.

### CrossOver: Phase II, [time estimate]

After-school programs will serve the needs of teenagers, including junior-high-school students, who will be invited to a variety of educational and recreational programs. These may include: homework assistance, computer lab, skate park, pick-up games of basketball or volleyball, clubs, Bible studies, practical-living courses, and so on.

The Gymworks Activity Center will be a gym with a large multipurpose area that will provide a place for basketball, volleyball, skating, and other large-group activities.

Discovery Zone will include smaller meeting rooms that will accommodate small-group gatherings simultaneous with large gatherings.

The Skate Park will be available for open skate times, lessons, birthday party rentals, competitions, and skate camps. This flexible space will be open to BMX bikes and in-line skates as well.

### Cross Training: Phase I, [time estimate]

In CrossTraining, teenagers will be integrated into the existing Community Church of Joy learning and growth opportunities, such as Teen Alpha, retreats, worship, and small-group ministries.

### Cross Training: Phase II, [time estimate]

These training and learning ministries will be expanded as The Crossing grows.

*CrossFire: Phase I, [time estimate]*

Teenagers will be equipped for leadership through current and expanded leadership development processes. Specialized training will be provided for those who are called to serve on The Crossing staff (both paid and volunteer).

*CrossFire: Phase II, [time estimate]*

A teen and young-adult training/mentoring process will be expanded for more extensive leadership development of teens, young-adult interns, and full-time staff.

## Attendance Projections

The projected attendance and anticipated level of participation in The Crossing programs are based upon several key factors, including the following:

- growth of current participation in Community Church of Joy teen programs and activities
- analysis of market potential, based upon teen population in the primary target area
- the significant impact of a highly visible and attractive place for teens
- expanded marketing and promotion of activities

## Program Fee Structure

While The Crossing will reach all teenagers and does not want personal financial constraints to become a barrier, most teens today have the capacity to pay for certain events or products. A generous scholarship program will support those who cannot pay.

Income will be received from the following:

- Special events: concerts, plays, dances, and other special events. For the type of music groups expected to play at The Crossing, we assume teens would typically pay [dollar amount]. Fees for dances and club nights will be minimal.

- Discount and full passes: annual discount passes for ongoing club events and activities (for example: concerts, dances). The success of this will depend upon positive connection with parents who anticipate regular contact by their children with The Crossing and are looking for a bargain. We anticipate in Year One that [number] teens will purchase discount cards and another fifty will purchase full passes.

- Food service: snacks, beverages, and meals sold at events and during hours when the club is open. In similar settings (for example: arcades, teen entertainment venues), during a two-hour visit, the average teenager spends $2 to $2.50 for food. We will assume spending of [dollar amount] per visit in Year One.

- Retail sales: T-shirts, books, tapes, and other teen-relevant items will be sold. This expenditure is typically not very high for teens, so we will estimate [dollar amount] per teen per visit.

- Video games: coin-operated, highly active video games. In similar settings, during a two-hour visit, an average teenager spends $2 to $4 on games. We will estimate [dollar amount] per teen per visit. Pool and table-tennis tables will be available at no charge.

- Facility rental: At times when The Crossing is not being utilized for teen activities, the space will be rented to groups from the Community Church of Joy (for example: singles, young adults, Joy School) and other community groups (for example: wedding receptions, other churches, school groups).

- School assemblies: The Crossing staff and interns will provide local schools with quality, character-based assemblies on teen issues. The honoraria will help offset the costs of the internship program.

## Program Evaluation

The programs and services of The Crossing will be evaluated in two ways. First, they will be evaluated according to the objectives and target dates set forth in this Operations Plan. Second, they will be evaluated according to the quality standards as guided by the values outlined in this plan.

The evaluation according to objectives and target dates will be measured with two methods:

1. We will gather and record attendance/participation data for each day of each event, program, or service. This data will be compiled on a monthly basis for review by the management team and will be included in The Crossing annual report.

2. The Teen Response Survey will create a starting-point baseline, against which survey results in future years will be measured. The Teen Response Survey will measure satisfaction levels and perceived behavioral changes by the teens and their families. Results will compare levels of participation and change in high-risk behaviors and growth, as well as other measurements set forth in the objectives. This may be tracked through a touch-screen computer kiosk in The Crossing.

The Teen Response Survey will also measure how well the values of The Crossing are being expressed by staff, mentors, volunteers, and other leaders. The survey will be conducted periodically, but participants will also be given tools to do immediate evaluations (for example: comment cards).

In addition to these participant evaluations, all staff and volunteers will be evaluated by the campuswide, 360-degree evaluation process that inspires improvement and affirms competencies and values that are vital to The Crossing's effectiveness and that of the entire mission.

## Organization and Staffing

### Governance

The Crossing will be governed by an Arizona 501(c)(3) nonprofit board of directors, with representation from the community and the church. Teens will be represented on the board of directors and on a Teen Council. Bylaws will ensure affiliation with the church as well as with the Joy Teen Ministry but also freedom to gain support from the community and legal/financial accountability as a distinct entity of the Community Church of Joy.

## Administrative Staffing

A development director will be hired one year prior to opening with the task of overseeing the development of Phase I. This person will focus on securing funding and assuring that the development plans and timetables are implemented.

An executive director will be hired at the appropriate time to oversee the vision and operation of The Crossing. This director will report to the board, hire and manage staff, maintain proper financial and legal accountability, and seek to promote The Crossing in the community and church, and among teens and other constituent groups.

As The Crossing grows, other administrative staff will be hired to lead and/or manage key areas (for example: food service, after-school programs).

## Program Staffing

Teams of paid and volunteer staff will be equipped to serve and lead teenagers in their faith journeys, as well as maintain the quality of The Crossing programs, services, and facilities. Staff members will enthusiastically function in a variety of roles as needed and will express the heart of The Crossing to all who come. These may be more mature teenagers, college students, interns, or young-adult volunteers from the church or community. The staff will also include one or more professionally trained counselors who specialize in the issues of teens and their families.

## Campus Services

Support services for The Crossing will be provided by the Joy Company Campus Services. These include housekeeping, maintenance, landscaping, human resources, marketing and public relations, fundraising, accounting, data processing, and technology support. Costs for these services along with utilities, insurance, and other campuswide costs will be funded through an appropriate inter-company allocation according to level of usage.

## Internship Opportunity

College-age students from Arizona and across the country will be invited to join the adventure of The Crossing by serving one year as Crossing intern staff. Each participant will benefit from specialized training in all aspects of youth leadership, including counseling skills, relationship-building skills, leadership dynamics, interventions, program development, music, drama, technology, missions, teaching, and mentoring. They also will form a support team that can help them process their experiences and grow personally as they serve.

Interns will receive only a small monthly stipend, so they will need to raise funds to supplement the stipend or depend on local families for room and board.

Internship candidates will apply and be screened based upon personal development, relational skills, compatibility with the vision and values of The Crossing, and their desire to learn, grow, and serve. The interns will also participate in the school assembly program two days each week.

## The Marketing/Communications Plan

## Market Analysis

According to the U.S. Census Bureau, there are 31.6 million teenagers (ages twelve to nineteen) living in the United States, and this number will grow to 34 million by the year 2010. This represents the largest generation since the baby boomers and constitutes a powerful force in our society. Within a five-mile radius of The Crossing, there are more than 30,000 teenagers, and this number will continue to grow at least through the year 2010.

## Teen Activities

On weekends, the largest segment of teenagers (48 percent) prefer to "hang out with friends" more than any other activity. A sense of belonging and acceptance is very important to them. The next-largest segment, 43 percent, prefer to "be with family" on weekends, while 35 percent watch television, 32 percent go to someone's house, and 25 percent like to go to a movie.[1]

Although no facility or program like The Crossing exists in our area, teens have always found something to do. Major competition for the time and resources of these teenagers includes movie theaters, malls, and activity centers, such as theme parks, skate parks, laser-tag venues, and water parks. Other options include church and school youth activities, sports training, sports events, music, drama, dancing, and other extracurricular school-related activities. Included in this competition would be fast-food hangouts, city parks, parks-and-recreation activities and sports, and various home entertainment options, such as video and cable movies, video and computer games, the Internet, and parties in the homes of teenagers.

## Teen Spending

The typical American teenager spends $56 per week of his/her own money, plus another $28 per week of family money on entertainment, food, and personal items, totaling $84 per week. The top items teenagers spend money on are as follows:

| Boys | | Girls | |
|---|---|---|---|
| compact disc | 58% | movie ticket | 60% |
| fast food | 57% | nail polish | 54% |
| movie ticket | 52% | chocolate candy | 53% |
| chocolate candy | 44% | compact disc | 53%[2] |

## Media Priorities

The advertising media that teens are most likely to pay attention to are the following:

| cable TV | 54% (MTV is the highest rated) |
| magazines | 53% |
| radio | 50% |
| movie screen ads | 48% |
| broadcast TV | 35% |

Eighty-one percent of teenagers use online service, with 61 percent using it at home and 53 percent at school. The Internet may become the primary vehicle for communicating with teens in the future.

## Marketing Goal

Our goal is to reach 5 percent of the teenagers in our primary target area (five-mile radius), or [number] teens per year by the end of the second year of operation and 10 percent per year by the fifth year of operation. We assume that the typical teen will participate an average of six times per year, so total participation by [year] is over [number] per year.

## What Differentiates The Crossing?

When teenagers were asked "What makes a brand cool?" their top five answers included (a) quality (63 percent), (b) for people my age (30 percent), (c) advertising (23 percent), (d) uniqueness (23 percent), and (e) cool friends or peers use it (20 percent). In its programs and market positioning, The Crossing has the opportunity to address all five of these priorities. The Crossing will be positioned as the "coolest" high-quality, value-based teen club in Arizona. A comprehensive marketing plan will be developed prior to opening, and marketing/communications efforts will be based on a more in-depth analysis.

## Marketing and Communications Strategy—Internal

Preliminary strategies for internal marketing and communications include staff efforts geared toward building a positive connection between The Crossing and the entire Community Church of Joy campus. These include the following.

*Communications Strategies*

- enthusiastic word-of-mouth communication by those who have participated in events and programs
- stories and endorsements by teenagers and interns in church newsletter and other in-house publications
- special events and orientations that welcome newcomers and their parents
- networking with other campus leaders to communicate the benefits of The Crossing

*Promotion Strategies*

- invitations distributed at campuswide events
- special promotions to teens and their families
- annual welcome events for preteens and their families
- monthly activity list included in church newsletter
- The Crossing internal database with newsletter for supporters, teens, and their families
- signage on The Crossing building and on street signs
- Web-site promotions

## Marketing and Communications Strategies—External

Preliminary strategies for external marketing and communications include efforts geared toward building a positive connection between The Crossing and the surrounding community. These include the following.

*Communications Strategies*

Crossing staff, interns, and volunteers will actively participate in other community activities and events to network relationships, create visibility for The Crossing, and demonstrate teamwork with the community at large. Specific communications strategies include:

- continuous press releases and stories for local newspapers
- networking with key school and community leaders
- networking with other church leaders who serve teenagers
- database and regular newsletter for all teens/families
- school assemblies sponsored by The Crossing

*Promotion Strategies*
- ads placed in every school newspaper and in school sports and music programs
- brochure in teen-oriented stores
- movie screen ads
- discount and annual passes
- tie-ins with local stores, malls, fast-food restaurants, theaters, sports events, concerts, and theme parks

## The Security Plan

Loitering is expected and welcomed at The Crossing. At the same time, well-enforced security is essential for the teens who frequent The Crossing and for their parents to feel secure in allowing them to come. There will be zero tolerance for violence, drugs, alcohol, and sexual promiscuity. A complete Security and Safety Policies, Procedures, and Training Guide will be developed by The Crossing staff. Security will be assured through the following means.

### Facilities and Technology
The Crossing facility is designed to maintain a secure environment through limited entrances and exits. While maintaining fire codes, staff will be able to allow teens to enter and exit the building through a limited number of doorways. For certain events, staff will be stationed at these doorways to check those who enter and exit. In addition, surveillance cameras will be used in

parts of the facility that do not have continuous exposure and visibility to the general public, so as to discourage unwanted activities. Signage will be utilized to clarify and emphasize The Crossing's safety rules and emergency procedures. These will be posted in highly visible locations.

## Parking Lot Security

During key events or high-participation times (for example: Friday nights after high-school games), well-trained staff and volunteer "parking lot greeters" will welcome teens and watch for negative activity. If these greeters suspect wrongful activity, having been trained how to respond, they will question the teens, inviting them to cease the activity, or will notify the police to respond. Skateboard activity will be allowed within designated areas.

## Pass Cards and Other Systems

Upon first entering The Crossing, each teen will complete an information card and receive a Crossing Pass, which allows the teens access to the facility. It also lists the schedule. They will also receive a brochure with the policies for safe and positive participation. These policies will indicate that if the person breaks the safety rules, he/she will be given one warning. With the next "infraction," he/she will be asked to leave and his/her card will be taken away for a period of time. The person can later reapply for another card.

The Crossing board will determine whether a pass-through metal detection device will be installed at the main entrances to The Crossing. This will be determined by perceived risk at the time.

## Emergency Procedures

In case of fire or other disaster, all staff and counselors, having received emergency training, will be able to lead the teens to safety. Medical personnel will be present at all large events, when the risk of medical emergencies is higher. The administrative staff will determine this policy.

## Security Personnel

Most important, all staff and volunteers will be trained to deal kindly and effectively with teenagers who cause problems for others. In addition, they will be trained in the essential safety policies and procedures. At key times (for example: concerts), extra, paid and volunteer security personnel will be enlisted to maintain security in the building and on the premises.

## THE FACILITY AND TECHNOLOGY PLAN

## Phase I Facilities

A large, open, multiuse, "warehouse"-type room with carpeted-floor seating for 800 to 1,000, theater style, also including:

- stage area (band and drama)
- video screens and sound system
- short-order food-service counter and prep area
- lounge area (couches, coffee tables, and so on)
- game area (variety of pool tables, video games, and so on)
- "cool" restrooms
- prayer rooms and smaller, counseling/meeting rooms
- office area
- retail counter for selling shirts, and so on
- secured outdoor patio with space for skateboarding, basketball, patio furniture, and outdoor concerts

## Phase II Facilities

A multiplex center for teen activities, including:

- games and entertainment
- gymnasium for concerts and sports activities
- counseling rooms
- expanded media connections
- expanded food service

- teen store
- more offices and work stations
- rooms and areas for seminars and classes

## Technology

Phase I will include:

- high-tech sound and lighting system
- video screens for music videos
- pool and table-tennis tables
- neon and electronic signage
- active sports-oriented video games
- touch-screen kiosks for teen feedback
- Crossing Web site accessible on site

Phase II will expand to include:

- computer stations for Internet searches, interactive learning, and studying
- expanded Web interaction from home
- facility maintenance

## Future Facility/Technology Innovation

In order to maintain its position as the cutting-edge teen club in this area, new technology, furnishings, and facility upgrades will be continually added. The leadership team will develop a process for assessing and developing innovative improvements.

## TIMETABLES

### Facility Development Timetable

| | |
|---|---|
| Complete Phase I Design | [Month, Year] |
| Complete Phase I Fundraising | [Month, Year] |

| | |
|---|---|
| Groundbreaking | [Month, Year] |
| Construction Completed | [Month, Year] |
| Move-In | [Month, Year] |
| Programs Begin | [Month, Year] |
| Dedication of Phase I | [Month, Year] |

## Operations Timetable

| | |
|---|---|
| Director Begins | [Month, Year] |
| Board of Directors Launched | [Month, Year] |
| Strategic Plan Approved | [Month, Year] |
| Staffing Plan Approved | [Month, Year] |
| Budget Approved | [Month, Year] |
| Program Planning | [Month, Year] |
| Marketing Planning | [Month, Year] |
| Marketing Campaign Launch | [Month, Year] |
| Interns/Volunteers Enlisted | [Month, Year] |
| Phase I Programming Begins | [Month, Year] |
| Phase II Programming Begins | [Month, Year] |

## THE FINANCIAL PLAN

### Capital Fund

Resources for the Phase I development of The Crossing facilities are being raised through a special "Crossing Campaign" among the members and friends of the Community Church of Joy. National and community leaders and organizations who believe in the mission and impact of The Crossing are also supporting the development with special gifts. The Phase I goal is to raise [dollar amount], plus in-kind gifts, to cover hard-and-soft development costs.

The Phase II goal is to raise [dollar amount] for a gymnasium, offices, game room, classrooms, and activity rooms.

## Phase I Operating Income

Operating funds for Phase I will come from the following three sources.

### Community Church of Joy Program Funds

The Joy Teen Ministry staff will continue to be funded through the operating budget of Community Church of Joy. They will collaborate extensively with The Crossing staff.

### Revenue from Operations

Several parts of Phase I of The Crossing will generate income through reasonable fees for: Crossing Café (food service), The Store, concert tickets, rentals for other functions and outside events (birthday parties), and other programs. Some of these programs will simply break even.

### Grants and Gifts

Special grants and gifts will be designated for operations and new programs (for example: counseling services, after-school programs). In addition, an endowment will be created to assist with the general overhead of the operations and need-based scholarships.

# A SAMPLE FUNDING PROPOSAL

## Putting Together a Grant Application

### Funding Proposal Submitted to the —— Foundation

This proposal is submitted by the Community Church of Joy to the ——
Foundation for consideration of a major gift to establish and develop The
Crossing, a facility designed to provide a safe, positive place for teenagers to
celebrate friendship with one another and to connect with God. The Crossing will attract teenagers in the community through entertainment, sports,
and food at an exciting venue that will create a contagious atmosphere.
Through the acceptance by peers and guidance of young-adult mentors, The
Crossing will support teens on their journey to become dynamic servant-
leaders in their community and the world.

### Overview

A growing body of data indicates that the United States is facing an increasing problem with inappropriate teenage behavior. Across the nation,

teenagers are engaging in activities that lead to delinquent behavior and eventual criminal activity. Statistics support the fact that teens involved in unwholesome activities cross socioeconomic boundaries and impact all cities, regardless of size.

A recent study contained in the *Sourcebook of Criminal Justice Statistics* identified serious teenage juvenile behavior affecting a large number of American teens. Of particular concern is the number of children who are becoming involved in serious criminal activity as a result of poor peer-group relationships and a distancing from family. These teenage behaviors impact all Americans in that they have a financial effect on every community that is struggling to find ways to deal with the problem.

The demand to find a better way to address teenage behavior and to develop a proactive method to interact with teens is well documented. Although there are individual efforts by some communities and agencies to develop teen programs, few address the key issue of providing a safe, positive environment in which teenagers are attracted to activity by positive peer-group interaction in an exciting and vibrant atmosphere. The Community Church of Joy will establish Arizona's first teen mall, The Crossing, to address these needs. The Crossing will serve as a prototype for communities across the country that seek to offer hope for teens.

## INTRODUCTION

The Community Church of Joy is a community-oriented, faith-based organization that has enjoyed unprecedented success in its twenty-five-year history. With more than fifteen thousand constituents, Community Church of Joy stands poised not only to develop new programs and activities that will benefit its community but also to share a model of success with other communities across the nation. The Community Church of Joy is passionately committed to sharing the love of God in relevant and engaging ways and to training and equipping people of all faith levels. The Community Church of

Joy continually seeks to create an inviting climate of warmth and hospitality that welcomes all who come.

The Community Church of Joy is committed to doing whatever it takes to build a community that reaches out to new people and helps them grow, by affirming and upholding the God-given worth of each individual. Out of this commitment grows a sincere desire to help people foster, build, and experience dynamic, vital relationships with one another. This commitment to people has resulted in the Community Church of Joy's establishing a successful preschool, K-8 school, school of performing arts, leadership-training programs presented across the nation, and development of a Leadership Center on the Community Church of Joy campus.

As an organization dedicated to needs-based solutions for real-people problems, the Community Church of Joy will implement and develop The Crossing to respond to the needs of teens in the Phoenix metro area. The Crossing will respond to research that identified an emerging regional and national need for a new and innovative approach to attract teens to a safe, positive environment for peer and adult-mentor interaction.

## NEEDS ASSESSMENT

National statistics, while showing a decline in inappropriate teenage behavior in some areas, overall indicates that, as a country, we are facing a serious problem surrounding teenage behavior. In the *Sourcebook of Criminal Justice Statistics Online,* national statistics are presented representing communities of all sizes across the United States.[1] A review of these statistics indicates that any given community is subject to a wide array of inappropriate and eventually criminal behavior. Metropolitan Phoenix, not unlike any other area of its size, is attempting to deal with juvenile-delinquency problems in much the same way as many other municipalities.

Today's children are growing up in an increasingly complex environment, where they don't even feel safe within their own peer groups. The *Sourcebook of Criminal Justice Statistics Online* indicates that 31 percent of teenagers reported being hit or beaten by someone their own age, and 19 percent reported being assaulted by an older teen. In the same study, 29 percent reported being a victim of a racial or ethnic insult, and 12 percent reported being attacked by a gang or posse.[2]

Coupled with the increase in concern for personal safety, teenagers are faced with ever-increasing amounts of unsupervised time, as a result of single working parents and families where both father and mother are working to support the household. This freedom, resulting from decreased parental supervision at home, creates opportunity for teens to become involved in substance abuse and increased sexual activity. The *Sourcebook of Criminal Justice Statistics Online* reveals that in large metropolitan cities such as Phoenix, 934 youths per 100,000 population are involved in drug abuse. The same study reveals that teen alcoholism rates reach 291 per 100,000 population.[3] When compared to the service area under consideration, there are as many as 2,335 teens involved in drug use and 727 teens abusing alcohol.

These statistics raise particular concern in relation to the rapid rate of growth of Arizona and the Southwest. Arizona has averaged a doubling of population every eighteen years during the past century. In the past decade, Arizona's growth rate percentage was exceeded nationally only by the state of Nevada, although Arizona's growth by total population was higher. In the past ten years, Arizona has grown by an amount exceeding the total population of Nebraska. Unfortunately, population growth in Arizona has been particularly robust in certain underserved areas where teen programs and intervention are in particular need. The Phoenix metro area, particularly the area near The Crossing, falls into this category.

## OBJECTIVES AND METHODS

Drawing on the established excellence for identifying and developing needs-based programs that make a commitment to the surrounding community, the Community Church of Joy will establish The Crossing to provide teens a place to cross from fear to faith, despair to hope, and loneliness to love. The mission of The Crossing is to provide an exciting, positive place for youth to celebrate friendships with one another free of fear. Teens in the community will be attracted to The Crossing through entertainment, sports, food, a contagious atmosphere, and the acceptance of peers and young-adult mentors.

The values for The Crossing will include:

- *Outreach.* The Crossing will seek intentional and creative ways to connect with teens in the broader community.
- *Transformation.* Centered in God's love, The Crossing will help teens experience the life-transforming power of faith in every area of life.
- *Hospitality.* The Crossing will welcome newcomers and active participants with open arms and acceptance in a nonthreatening atmosphere.
- *A positive "vibe."* The Crossing will have a positive vibe through the use of creative lighting, color, sound, music, and, most important, the positive attitude of the staff.
- *Relational values.* Programs and facilities will serve as doorways to relationships, with a high ratio of paid/volunteer staff to participants who will "hang out" with the teens.
- *Empowered volunteers.* Empowered and equipped volunteers who are passionately involved in their faith and sincerely desire to positively affect teens will express their genuine joy through their words and actions.
- *Teen leadership.* The leadership potential of all teens will be encouraged and nurtured, as they help guide the direction of The Crossing.
- *Quality.* The programs, services, food, and facilities of The Crossing will reflect the high quality that attracts teens and encourages them to invite their friends.
- *Integrity.* The staff and volunteers of The Crossing will integrate high ethical values with their everyday discussions and actions.

- *Character-based development.* Character-based leadership will model and train a values approach to problem solving.
- *Safety.* Teens and their parents will be confident that The Crossing will provide a safe, secure environment, free of drugs, alcohol, sexual activity, and violence.
- *Diversity.* The Crossing will connect with the wide variety of interests and needs of teens in the community.

## Who We Will Serve

Primary audience: twelve- to nineteen-year-olds who live within a twenty-five-mile radius of The Crossing.

Secondary audiences: teens throughout the Phoenix metropolitan area, as well as parents of teens who participate in Crossing programs.

National audiences: young adults who want to develop leadership skills in working with teens and their families, as well as leaders across the country who are searching for a high-impact model to reach teens in their own communities.

## The Goals

**Goal I: to attract a multitude of teens to The Crossing.**
Our objectives include drawing the following numbers of teenagers:
- [number] teen participants per year by [year]

To achieve this objective, we will pursue the following strategies:
- momentum-building events that encourage teens to invite friends
- need-meeting programs
- dynamic staff who build one-to-one relationships with teens
- ongoing community marketing/PR, targeting teens and their parents
- developing a first-class facility and amenities that will attract large numbers of teenagers

## Goal II: to care for the spiritual, emotional, mental, and physical needs of teenagers.

Our objectives include providing specific services and ministries to the following numbers of teenagers:

- [number] teens will receive personal care/mentoring each year by [year]
- [number] teen participants per year will report reduced personal, negative, or substance-abuse activities by [year]

To achieve these objectives, we will pursue the following strategies:

- programs that inspire and assist teens in the development of their whole lives—faith, intellect, physical fitness, relationships, and personal well-being
- strategic alliances with the overall mission of the Community Church of Joy and other dynamic teen-based service organizations
- intervention for teens in need

## Goal III: to invite teenagers to a relationship with God and the faith community.

Our objectives include the following outcomes and ministries:

- [number] teenagers per year to express new faith foundations through a Crossing program by [year]
- [number] teens per year to report new involvement in a faith community by [year]

To achieve these objectives, we will pursue the following strategies:

- introduction to faith, which will be integrated into ongoing programs and events
- intentional assimilation of teenagers and their families into the broader life of area churches

## Goal IV: to support healthy relationships between teens and their family members, their peers, and their community.

Our objectives include the following outcomes and ministries:

- [number] parents per year to participate in Crossing programs by [year]

- [number] teenagers and parents to report improved relationships in their families through programs of The Crossing by [year]
- [number] teens to report improved relationships with peers through programs of The Crossing by [year]

To achieve these objectives, we will pursue the following strategies:

- parent-teen relationship-building programs and activities
- parent involvement in leadership and service for Crossing programs
- peer relationship building as part of ongoing programs

## Goal V: to equip teenagers to become lifelong learners and servant-leaders.

Our objectives include the following outcomes and ministries:

- [number] teens participating in some type of spiritual growth/service activity by [year]
- [number] teens per year to report involvement in some type of leadership role by [year]

To achieve these objectives, we will pursue the following strategies:

- high-energy, relational learning environments, such as small groups, classes, and large-group presentations, utilizing many forms of media and art
- leadership-training track
- process for helping teens explore their personal passion and gifts

## Goal VI: The Crossing organization will positively impact its local, regional, and national communities.

Our objectives include the following outcomes and ministries:

- [number] schools or community groups to be served each year with quality, character-based substance-abuse and sexuality-awareness seminars by [year]
- [number] local teens each year to be equipped with job and leader-

ship skills so they can positively contribute to society in their current and future careers by [year]

- Crossing volunteers to assist in two or more major community-improvement activities each year by [year]
- [number] financially challenged teenagers and their families to be served by The Crossing staff and volunteers each year by [year]
- [number] organizations across the country to receive assistance from The Crossing each year in their own community outreaches to teenagers

To achieve these objectives, we will pursue the following strategies:

- substance-abuse-awareness assemblies in local schools and community seminars at The Crossing
- sexuality-awareness assemblies in local schools and community seminars at The Crossing
- job fairs and career-development seminars at The Crossing
- special programs to adopt/assist needy families that include teenage members
- annual community-improvement project (for example: park cleanup)
- collaboration with other teen-oriented, community-service organizations
- materials, Web sites, consulting, and other resources to assist churches and community organizations in visioning and developing their outreaches to teenagers

## The Program Plan

### Program Components for CrossOver, Phase I, [Time Estimate]

This is a wide-open door where teens can come in and "cross over" from the world into an atmosphere of celebration, grace, acceptance, and unconditional love. The staff (both paid and volunteer) will seek to build relationships in order to earn the right to be heard by teenagers.

The Crossing Club is the central place that embraces teens and meets their broad social, recreational, and entertainment needs. Through music, videos, pool tables, interactive video games, a place to hang out, and great food, teens invite their friends into this clubhouse environment. Well-trained staff will ensure a safe environment and will reach out to those who attend with love and friendship rather than just policing the area as "chaperones." There will be concerts, dances, theater presentations, battle-of-the-band nights, and more. Whatever is on the edge and attracts teens in a wholesome way will be considered.

Another important component will be performing arts and visual arts. Not only will the arts serve as an integral part of the presentations for teens, but teenagers also will perform and tour with the traveling music and drama teams. Opportunities for multiple expressions of the visual arts also will be incorporated into the program.

Special off-site events will include trips to California theme parks and amusement parks, overnight trips, ski trips, mission and service projects, and other events, all providing great opportunities for active youth to invite their friends.

Seminars, classes, and workshops will focus on faith issues and practical-living topics.

Crisis help and counseling will provide a safe place and support for at-risk teens. Teenagers will be assisted by caring professionals to discover or sustain a positive, drug-free life.

The Crossing interns will develop a high-energy "character-development" themed program for presentation two days each week in public schools. These assemblies are funded by a government grant. They will give tremendous exposure to The Crossing and its staff.

### CrossOver: Phase II, [Time Estimate]

After-school programs will serve the needs of teenagers, including junior-high-school students, who will be invited to a variety of educational and recreational programs. These may include: homework assistance, computer lab, skate park, pick-up games of basketball or volleyball, clubs, Bible studies, practical-living courses, and so on.

The Gymworks Activity Center will be a gym with a large multipurpose area that will provide a place for basketball, volleyball, skating, and other large-group activities.

Discovery Zone will include smaller meeting rooms that will accommodate small-group gatherings simultaneous with large gatherings.

The Skate Park will be available for open skate times, lessons, birthday party rentals, competitions, and skate camps. This flexible space will be open to BMX bikes and in-line skates as well.

## CrossTraining: Phase I, [Time Estimate]

In CrossTraining, teenagers will be integrated into the existing Community Church of Joy learning and growth opportunities, such as Teen Alpha, retreats, worship, and small-group ministries.

## CrossFire: Phase I, [Time Estimate]

Teenagers will be equipped for leadership through current and expanded leadership development processes. Specialized training will be provided for those who are called to serve on The Crossing staff (both paid and volunteer).

## CrossFire: Phase II, [Time Estimate]

A teen and young-adult training/mentoring process will be expanded for more extensive leadership development of teens, young-adult interns, and full-time staff.

## PROGRAM FEE STRUCTURE

While The Crossing will reach all teenagers and does not want personal financial constraints to become a barrier, most teens today have the capacity to pay for certain events or products. A generous scholarship program will support those who cannot pay.

Income will be received from the following:

- Special events: concerts, plays, dances, and other special events. For the type of music groups expected to play at The Crossing, we assume teens would typically pay [dollar amount]. Fees for dances and club nights will be minimal.

- Discount and full passes: annual discount passes for ongoing club events and activities (for example: concerts, dances). The success of this will depend upon positive connection with parents who anticipate regular contact by their children with The Crossing and are looking for a bargain. We anticipate in Year One that fifty teens will purchase discount cards and another fifty will purchase full passes.

- Food service: snacks, beverages, and meals sold at events and during hours when the club is open. In similar settings (for example: arcades, teen entertainment venues), during a two-hour visit, the average teenager spends $2 to $2.50 for food. We will assume spending of [dollar amount] per visit in Year One.

- Retail sales: T-shirts, books, tapes, and other teen-relevant items will be sold. This expenditure is typically not very high for teens, so we will estimate [dollar amount] per teen per visit.

- Video games: coin-operated, highly active video games. In similar settings, during a two-hour visit, an average teenager spends $2 to $4 on games. We will estimate [dollar amount] per teen per visit. Pool and table-tennis tables will be available at no charge.

- Facility rental: At times when The Crossing is not being utilized for teen activities, the space will be rented to groups from the Community Church of Joy (for example: singles, young adults, Joy School) and other community groups (for example: wedding receptions, other churches, school groups).

- School assemblies: The Crossing staff and interns will provide local schools with quality, character-based assemblies on teen issues. The honoraria will help offset the costs of the internship program.

## Attendance Projections

The projected attendance and anticipated level of participation in The Crossing programs are based upon several key factors, including the following:

- growth of current participation in Community Church of Joy teen programs and activities
- analysis of market potential, based upon teen population in the primary target area
- the significant impact of a highly visible and attractive place for teens
- expanded marketing and promotion of activities

## Program Evaluation

The programs and services of The Crossing will be evaluated in two ways. First, they will be evaluated according to the objectives and target dates set forth in the Operations Plan. Second, they will be evaluated according to the quality standards as guided by the values outlined in this plan.

The evaluation according to objectives and target dates will be measured with two methods:

1. We will gather and record attendance/participation data for each day of each event, program, or service. This data will be compiled on a monthly basis for review by the management team and will be included in The Crossing annual report.

2. The Survey will create a starting-point baseline, against which survey results in future years will be measured. The Teen Response Survey will measure satisfaction levels and perceived behavioral changes by teens and their families. Results will compare levels of participation and change in high-risk behaviors and growth, as well as other measurements set forth in the objectives. This may be tracked through a touch-screen computer kiosk in The Crossing.

The Teen Response Survey will also measure how well the values of The Crossing are being expressed by staff, mentors, volunteers, and other leaders. The survey will be conducted periodically, but participants will also be given tools to do immediate evaluations (for example: comment cards).

In addition to these participant evaluations, all staff and volunteers will be evaluated by the campuswide, 360-degree evaluation process that inspires improvement and affirms competencies and values that are vital to The Crossing's effectiveness and that of the entire mission.

## TIMETABLES

### Facility Development Timetable

| | |
|---|---|
| Complete Phase I Design | [Month, Year] |
| Complete Phase I Fundraising | [Month, Year] |
| Groundbreaking | [Month, Year] |
| Construction Completed | [Month, Year] |
| Move-In | [Month, Year] |
| Programs Begin | [Month, Year] |
| Dedication of Phase I | [Month, Year] |

### Operations Timetable

| | |
|---|---|
| Director Begins | [Month, Year] |
| Board of Directors Launched | [Month, Year] |

| | |
|---|---|
| Strategic Plan Approved | [Month, Year] |
| Staffing Plan Approved | [Month, Year] |
| Budget Approved | [Month, Year] |
| Program Planning | [Month, Year] |
| Marketing Planning | [Month, Year] |
| Marketing Campaign Launch | [Month, Year] |
| Interns/Volunteers Enlisted | [Month, Year] |
| Phase I Programming Begins | [Month, Year] |
| Phase II Programming begins | [Month, Year] |

## THE FINANCIAL PLAN

### Capital Fund

Resources for the Phase I development of The Crossing facilities are being raised through a special "Crossing Campaign" among the members and friends of the Community Church of Joy. Community leaders and organizations that believe in the mission and impact of The Crossing are also supporting the development with special gifts. The Phase I goal is to raise [dollar amount] in cash, plus in-kind gifts for facility hard-and-soft development costs.

The Phase II goal is [dollar amount] for a gymnasium, offices, game room, classrooms, and activity rooms.

### Phase I Operating Income

Operating funds for Phase I will come from three sources:

#### *Community Church of Joy Program Funds*

The Joy Teen Ministry staff will continue to be funded through the operating budget of Community Church of Joy. They will collaborate extensively with The Crossing staff.

*Revenue from Operations*

Several parts of Phase I of The Crossing will generate income through reasonable fees for: Crossing Café (food service), The Store, concert tickets, rentals for other functions and outside events (birthday parties), and other programs. Some of these programs will simply break even.

*Grants and Gifts*

Special grants and gifts will be designated for operations and new programs (for example: counseling services, after-school programs). In addition, an endowment will be created to assist with the general overhead of the operations and need-based scholarships.

## An Invitation to Partnership

Basic to the initiation and growth of The Crossing is the development of funding to provide for facility design and construction, program development, technology components, basic capital costs, and developmental costs to prepare and disseminate information to other communities on the effectiveness of The Crossing.

We are seeking a leadership gift distributed over three years from the —— Foundation to assist us in implementing this innovative and far-reaching facility to provide teens a safe, positive community atmosphere in which to enjoy fellowship and to grow as young adults. The advocacy of the —— Foundation, evidenced through your commitment to youth, will be a significant factor in the successful advancement of The Crossing. The Community Church of Joy welcomes your consideration and commitment for this historic enterprise as follows:

- Year One: A gift of [dollar amount] to assist in the development and construction of the facility.
- Year Two: A gift of [dollar amount] to establish operations and

technology infrastructures, implement programs, establish feed-back mechanisms, and evaluate program effectiveness.

- Year Three: A gift of [dollar amount] to modify programs based on feedback and to develop methods of program dissemination to share with other communities across the nation, including but not limited to an Internet site with streaming video and contact information.

## SUMMARY

An increasing body of evidence indicates that the United States is facing a growing problem with inappropriate teenage behavior. Across the nation, teens are engaging in activities that lead to delinquent behavior and eventual criminal activity. Statistics support the fact that teens involved in unwholesome activities cross socioeconomic boundaries, and this trend affects all of our cities, regardless of size. Of particular concern is the number of children who are becoming involved in serious criminal activity as a result of poor peer-group relationships and a distancing from family. These teenage behaviors impact all Americans in that they have a financial effect on every community that is struggling to find ways to deal with the problem.

Although there are individual efforts by some communities and agencies to develop teen programs, few address the key issue of providing a safe, positive, faith-based environment in which teens are attracted to activity by positive peer-group interaction in an exciting and vibrant atmosphere. The Crossing will address this need by implementing and developing Arizona's first teen mall.

The Crossing is seeking a leadership gift from the —— Foundation to be distributed over a three-year period for construction, program development, and program dissemination to other communities across the nation that wish to address teen problems in an innovative, safe, and proactive environment.

# NOTES

## Introduction

1. "American Religious Identification Survey," 2001, The Graduate Center, The City University of New York, 365 Fifth Avenue, New York, NY, 10016, www.gc.cuny.edu/studies/key_findings.htm.

2. Robert Putnam, *Bowling Alone: The Collapse and Revival of American Community* (New York: Simon & Schuster, 2000), 71.

3. Barna Research Group, "Twentysomethings Struggle to Find Their Place in Christian Churches," September 24, 2003, www.barna.org.

4. Barna, "Twentysomethings Struggle."

## Chapter 1

1. Kirbyjon Caldwell, *The Gospel of Good Success* (New York: Simon & Schuster, 1999).

## Chapter 2

1. Kennon Callahan, *Effective Church Leadership: Building on the Twelve Keys* (Hoboken, NJ: Jossey-Bass, 1997).

## Chapter 3

1. See Joseph A. Schumpeter, *The Theory of Economic Development: An Inquiry into Profits, Capital, Credit, Interest and the Business Cycle,* trans. R. Ople (Cambridge, MA.: Harvard University Press, 1934).

## Chapter 5

1. For more of the Bethel New Life story, see www.bethelnewlife.org/about.html.

2. Kiwanis International, 2004, www.kiwanis.org/about/history/.

3. Robert Putnam and Lewis Feldstein, *Better Together: Restoring the American Community* (New York: Simon & Schuster, 2003), 4.

4. Putnam and Feldstein, *Better Together,* 4.

5. Robert Putnam, *Bowling Alone: The Collapse and Revival of American Community* (New York: Simon & Schuster, 2000), 67.

## Chapter 6

1. From a roundtable conversation with Margaret Wheatley and Paul Sorensen in Scottsdale, Arizona, 9–11 October, 2003.

## Chapter 8

1. Gene Kranz, *Failure Is Not an Option: Mission Control from Mercury to Apollo 13 and Beyond* (New York: Simon & Schuster, 2000), 1.

## Chapter 9

1. See Dauril Alden, *The Making of an Enterprise: The Society of Jesus in Portugal, Its Empire, and Beyond, 1540–1750* (Stanford: Stanford University Press, 1996).

2. See William Danker, *Profit for the Lord: Economic Activities in Moravian Missions and the Basel Mission Trading Company* (Grand Rapids: Eerdmanns, 1971).

## Chapter 10

1. See Herbert Lockyer, *All the Apostles of the Bible* (Grand Rapids: Zondervan, 1972).

## Chapter 11

1. See Peter Greig, *Red Moon Rising* (Lake St. Mary, FL: Relevant, 2003).

2. For the complete story on the 24-7 prayer movement, see Peter Greig, *Red Moon Rising,* or visit the Web site at www.24-7prayer.com.

3. For more on this idea, see Donald Miller, *Blue Like Jazz: Nonreligious Thoughts on Christian Spirituality* (Nashville, TN: Nelson, 2003).

## Chapter 12

1. See John Eldredge, *Wild at Heart: Discovering the Secret of a Man's Soul* (Nashville, TN: Nelson, 2001).

## Chapter 14

1. Frederick Nohl, *Luther: Biography of a Reformer* (St. Louis, MO: Concordia, 2003), 107.

## Chapter 15

1. Arthur Pell, *The Complete Idiot's Guide to Team Building* (Indianapolis, IN: Alpha, 1999).

## Chapter 17

1. Quoted in George Gendron, "The Hottest Entrepreneur in America?" May 1, 1996, *Inc* magazine.
2. World Christian Database, Center for the Study of Global Christianity, Gordon-Conwell Theological Seminary, 130 Essex Street, South Hamilton, MA, 01982, www.gem-werc.org.

## Chapter 19

1. Look again at Kirbyjon's story in chapter 1.
2. Look again at Walt's story in chapter 2.
3. "It Don't Come Easy," lyrics and music by Ringo Starr (London: Abbey Road, 1970).
4. Napoleon Hill, *Think and Grow Rich* (Meriden, CT: Ralston Society, 1937).

## Chapter 20

1. See John Maxwell, *Failing Forward: Turning Mistakes into Stepping-Stones for Success* (Nashville, TN: Nelson, 2000).

## Chapter 21

1. Quoted in Robert Putnam and Lewis Feldstein, *Better Together: Restoring the American Community* (New York: Simon & Schuster, 2003), 127.

## Chapter 22

1. Adapted from Adelaide Pollard, "Have Thine Own Way, Lord," music by George C. Stebbins. Public domain.

2. Adapted from Walt Kallestad, *Wake Up Your Dreams: A Proven Strategy to Help You Discover Your Lifelong Dream* (Grand Rapids: Zondervan, 1998).

## Chapter 23

1. Mike Martz, quoted in *Time* magazine.

2. National Football League, 2004, www.nfl.com/teams/coaching/STL.

## Appendix A

1. Jeffry Timmons, *New Venture Creation: Entrepreneurship for the 21*ˢᵗ *Century* (Boston: McGraw-Hill, 1999), 80.

## Appendix B

1. *Sourcebook of Criminal Justice Statistics Online, Sourcebook 2002,* http://albany.edu/sourcebook/1995.

## Appendix C

1. This research was gathered from Teen Research Unlimited, as cited in Peter Zollo, *Wise Up to Teens* (Ithaca, NY: New Strategist, 1999).

2. Teen Research Unlimited, as cited in Zollo, *Wise Up.*

## Appendix D

1. *Sourcebook,* http://albany.edu/sourcebook/1995.

2. *Sourcebook,* http://albany.edu/sourcebook/1995.

3. *Sourcebook,* http://albany.edu/sourcebook/1995.

# RECOMMENDED READING

For further reading on entrepreneurship and the life of the entrepreneur, we suggest the following:

Abery, J., A. Barber, J. Brown, P. Cullum, V. Datta, S. Gear, et al. *Liberating the Entrepreneurial Spirit.* London: Accenture Policy and Corporate Affairs.

Alden, Dauril. *The Making of an Enterprise: The Society of Jesus in Portugal, Its Empire, and Beyond, 1540-1750.* Stanford: Stanford University Press, 1996.

Barman, Emily. "Asserting Difference: The Strategic Response of Non-profit Organization to Competition." *Social Forces* 80, no. 4 (2002): 1191-1222.

Barna, George. *Building Effective Lay Leadership Teams.* Ventura, CA: Issachar Resources, 2001.

Bennis, Warren, and Joan Goldsmith. *Learning to Lead: A Workbook on Becoming a Leader.* Reading, MA: Perseus, 1997.

Bilodeau, Marc. "Rational Nonprofit Entrepreneurship." *Journal of Economics & Management Strategy* 7, (1998): 551-72.

Blanchard, Ken, and Sheldon Bowles. *High Five! The Magic of Working Together.* New York: Morrow, 2000.

Blanchard, Ken, and Phil Hodges. *The Servant Leader: Transforming Your Heart, Head, Hands and Habits.* Nashville, TN: J. Countryman, 2003.

Blanchard, Ken, Bill Hybels, and Phil Hodges. *Leadership by the Book: Tools to Transform Your Workplace.* New York: Morrow, 1999.

Boone, Mary. *Managing Interactively: Executing Business Strategy, Improving Communication, and Creating a Knowledge-Sharing Culture.* New York: McGraw-Hill, 2001.

Bossidy, Larry, and Ram Charan. *Execution: The Discipline of Getting Things Done.* New York: Crown Business, 2002.

Brinckerhoff, Peter. *Social Entrepreneurship: The Art of Mission-Based Venture Development.* New York: Wiley, 2000.

Caldwell, Kirbyjon. *The Gospel of Good Success.* New York: Simon & Schuster, 1999.

Christensen, Clayton. *The Innovator's Dilemma: When New Technologies Cause Great Companies to Fail.* New York: HarperBusiness, 2002.

Collins, Jim. *Good to Great: Why Some Companies Make the Leap and Others Don't.* New York: HarperBusiness, 2001.

Cunningham, J. Barton, and Joe Lischeron. "Defining Entrepreneurship." *Journal of Small Business Management* 29: 45-62.

Danker, William. *Profit for the Lord: Economic Activities in Moravian Missions and the Basel Mission Trading Company.* Grand Rapids: Eerdmanns, 1971.

Dees, Gregory. "Enterprising Nonprofits: Move by Nonprofit Organizations to 'Commercialize' Their Fund Raising Activities." *Harvard Business Review* 76, no. 1 (1998): 55-66.

———. "Linking Corporate Entrepreneurship to Strategy, Structure, and Process: Suggested Research Directions." *Entrepreneurship: Theory & Practice* 23 (1999): 85-103.

Dees, Gregory, Jed Emerson, and Peter Economy. *Enterprising Nonprofits: A Toolkit for Social Entrepreneurs.* New York: Wiley, 2001.

———. *Strategic Tools for Social Entrepreneurs: Enhancing the Performance of Your Enterprising Nonprofit.* New York: Wiley, 2002.

Dodd, Sarah, and Paul Seaman. "Religion and Enterprise: An Introductory Exploration." *Entrepreneurship: Theory & Practice* 23, no. 1 (1998): 71-86.

Drucker, Peter. *Innovation and Entrepreneurship: Practices and Principles.* New York: Harper & Row, 1985.

———. *Managing the Nonprofit Organization: Practices and Principles.* New York: HarperCollins, 1990.

———. *Management Challenges for the 21ˢᵗ Century.* New York: HarperBusiness, 1999.

Easum, Bill, and William M. Easum. *Leadership on the Other Side: No Rules, Just Clues.* Nashville, TN: Abingdon, 2000.

Eisner, Michael. *Michael Eisner: Work in Progress.* New York: Random House, 1998.

Ekelund, Robert, Robert Hebert, and Robert Tollison. "An Economic Analysis of the Protestant Reformation." *Journal of Political Economy* 110, no. 3 (2002): 646-61.

Fondation, Larry, Peter Tufano, and Patricia Walker. "Collaborating with Congregations." *Harvard Business Review* 77, no. 4 (1999): 57-66.

Freiberg, Kevin, and Jackie Freiberg. *Nuts: Southwest Airlines' Crazy Recipe for Business and Personal Success.* Austin, TX: Bard, 1996.

Fullan, Michael. *Leading in a Culture of Change.* San Francisco: Jossey-Bass, 2001.

Galaskiewicz, Joseph, and Wolfgang Bielefeld. "Nonprofits in an Age of Uncertainty: A Study of Organizational Change." *Independent Sector: Facts and Findings* 2, no. 1 (2002). www.independent sector.org.

Gates, William. *Business at the Speed of Thought: Succeeding in the Digital Economy.* New York: Warner, 2000.

Goleman, Daniel, Richard Boyatzis, and Annie McKee. *Primal Leadership: Realizing the Power of Emotional Intelligence.* Boston: Harvard Business School Press, 2002.

Hesselbein, Frances, Marshall Goldsmith, and Richard Beckhard, eds. *The Drucker Foundation: The Organization of the Future,* San Francisco: Jossey-Bass, 1997.

Hoge, Dean, Charles Zech, Patrick McNamara, and Michael Dona-hue. "The Value of Volunteers as Resources for Congregations." *Journal for the Scientific Study of Religion* 37, no. 3 (1998): 470-80.

Kallestad, Walt. *Be Your Own Creative Coach: Unlocking the Power of Your Imagination to Revolutionize Your Relationships, Career and Future.* Grand Rapids: Zondervan, 1998.

———. *Turn Your Church Inside Out: Building a Community for Others.* Minneapolis: Augsburg Fortress, 2001.

Kotter, John. *Leading Change.* Boston: Harvard Business School Press, 1996.

Kottler, Jeffrey. *Making Changes Last.* Philadelphia: Brunner-Routledge, 2001.

Love, John. *McDonald's: Behind the Golden Arches.* New York: Bantam, 1995.

McGrath, Rita, and Ian MacMillan. *The Entrepreneurial Mindset: Strategies for Continuously Creating Opportunity in an Age of Uncertainty.* Boston: Harvard Business School Press, 2000.

Morgan, Gareth. *Images of Organization.* Thousand Oaks, CA: Sage, 1997.

Morley, Elaine, Elisa Vinson, and Harry Hatry. "Outcome Measurement in Nonprofit Organizations: Current Practices and Recommendations." *The Independent Sector and the Urban Institute* (2001). www.independentsector.org.

Oster, Merrill, Mike Hamil, and Bill Bright. *The Entrepreneur's Creed: The Principles and Passions of 20 Successful Entrepreneurs.* Nashville, TN: Broadman & Holman, 2001.

Peters, Tom. *The Circle of Innovation: You Can't Shrink Your Way to Greatness.* New York: Knopf, 1997.

Putman, Robert. *Bowling Alone: The Collapse and Revival of American Community.* New York: Simon & Schuster, 2002.

Reiss, Alvin. "The Hidden Economy: The Nonprofit Sector." *Management Review* 78, no. 7 (1989): 49-51.

Reynolds, Paul, et al. "The Entrepreneur Next Door: Characteristics of Individuals Starting Companies in America." *A Report Sponsored by the Ewing Marion Kauffman Foundation,* 2002. www.emkf.org/pages/316.ofm.

Ryan, William. "The New Landscape for Nonprofits." *Harvard Business Review* 77, no. 1 (1999): 127.

Saxon-Harrold, Susan, Susan Wiener, Michael McCormack, and Michelle Weber. "America's Religious Congregations: Measuring Their Contribution to Society." *Independent Sector,* Measures Project (2001). www.independentsector.org.

Schaller, Lyle. *The Very Large Church: New Rules for Leaders.* Nashville, TN: Abingdon, 2000.

Senge, Peter. *The Fifth Discipline: The Art and Practice of the Learning Organization.* New York: Doubleday Currency, 1990.

Slaughter, Michael. *Spiritual Entrepreneurs: 6 Principles for Risking Renewal.* Nashville, TN: Abingdon, 1995.

Stebbins, Michael. "Business, Faith and the Common Good." *Review of Business* 19, no. 1 (1997): 5-9.

Thomas, Bob. *Building a Company: Roy O. Disney and the Creation of an Entertainment Empire.* New York: Hyperion, 1998.

Timmons, Jeffry. *New Venture Creation: Entrepreneurship for the 21$^{st}$ Century.* Boston: Irwin McGraw-Hill, 1999.

Walton, Sam. *Sam Walton, Made in America: My Story.* New York: Doubleday, 1992.

Wheatley, Margaret. *Leadership and the New Science: Discovering Order in a Chaotic World.* San Francisco: Berrett-Koehler, 1999.

Zimmermann, Horst. "Innovation in Nonprofit Organizations." *Annals of Public and Cooperative Economics* 70, no. 4 (1999): 589-620.

253
C1476

109953

LINCOLN CHRISTIAN COLLEGE AND SEMINARY

3 4711 00222 6902